I Almost Quit

Leading Through the Landmines of Ministry

Published by El Paseo Publications

Printed in the United States of America

Scripture is taken from the New King James Version®. Copyright © 1982 by Thomas Nelson. Used by permission. All rights reserved. Scriptures and quotes within quotation marks are exact quotes, whereas paraphrased Scriptures and quotes are often italicized.

Scripture quotations marked (NIV) are taken from the Holy Bible, New International Version®, NIV®. Copyright © 1973, 1978, 1984, 2011 by Biblica, Inc.™ Used by permission of Zondervan. All rights reserved worldwide. www.zondervan.com The "NIV" and "New International Version" are trademarks registered in the United States Patent and Trademark Office by Biblica, Inc.™

ISBN-13: 978-1-7343774-5-3

Acknowledgements: A very special thank you to my wife, Morgan; this book would have never been published without her support. And thank you to my wonderful kids who have made pastoring such a blessing: Aubrey, Shane, Gracie, Kylee, and Madison.

And a big thank you to the wonderful congregation of *Westside Christian Fellowship* in Southern California. I also want to acknowledge Christine Ramsey for her incredible editing skills and suggestions, along with Luis Arellano for the cover design and Cassia Watts for interior design.

Special Note: Internet links are current up to the printing date. Neither the author nor the publisher endorses all the book's references from outside sources. Related links are provided for eBook users — simply click the embedded link. If you are reading the printed version of this book, you will need to manually input the link into your browser.

Table of Contents

Important Introduction...9

Chapter One: Why I Almost Quit......................................15

Chapter Two: The Shepherds Have Become Dull-hearted.....31

Chapter Three: Winning the War Within.........................45

Chapter Four: Pride's Explosion is Far-Reaching.................57

Chapter Five: God Breaks You to Remake You...................73

Chapter Six: Poor Health Hinders Productivity..................85

Chapter Seven: Morgan Idleman — I Almost Quit Too.........99

Conclusion...119

Recommended Reading..123

Important Introduction

Leading Through the Landmines of Ministry

Important Introduction

The reasons you may have picked up this book are vast — some may be experiencing amazing growth as well as spiritual and physical health, while other readers are barely holding on. Pastoring is a hard calling because our lives and the lives of our wives and children are constantly on display for the world to see. Because we are guarded and cautious, we are often labeled prideful, arrogant, and distant. **But the truth is that we've been hurt so much that the walls we build to protect ourselves can eventually imprison us.**

Trusted friends leave, fellow believers turn away, and the enemy of our soul assaults our families. Sermons are scrutinized, inspected, and rejected by a small band of critics. Our services are judged as either too conservative by the highly emotional or too expressive by the armchair theologian.

The "Critical-Kathys" and "Judgmental-Jerrys" quickly let us know if we spend too much time in the Old Testament, talk too much about revival, or focus too much on the work of the Holy Spirit. When we dare touch on political hot buttons, we're quickly labeled as either too political or not political enough. The criticism never ends. I'm not trying to be negative; I'm being realistic.

Studies by Barna show that church-goers expect their pastor to juggle an average of 16 major tasks. Barna continues: "That's a recipe for failure — nobody can handle the wide range of responsibilities that people expect pastors to master."[1] But there is hope! Keep reading.

When the Dream Dies

During the beginning stages of pastorings, most of us are full of hope and enthusiasm. Later in life, depression can easily set in because of missed opportunities, slow growth, offenses, hurt, bitterness, slander, and even poor health. For some, you are living your dream, but for others, your dream has died. But one thing, and one thing only, keeps us going: *God has called us.*

As most know, a landmine is a concealed explosive device usually camouflaged in the ground. The purpose is to destroy or disable people as they pass by. What incredible spiritual imagery of Satan's goal — to destroy and disable our testimony and our leadership.

After reading many articles and listening to interviews about fallen leaders, it's clear that they fell because their pursuit of God was compromised. Our pursuit of God encompasses our

---

[1] https://www.barna.com/research/a-profile-of-protestant-pastors-in-anticipation-of-pastor-appreciation-month/

efforts to draw near to Him through prayer, worship, study of Scripture, obedience, and other spiritual disciplines. In the case of fallen leaders, their passion for God was no longer a burning desire but a flickering flame. *The greatest hindrance to drawing near to God is our satisfaction without Him.* Obviously, there are other landmines in the field of ministry that hinder our calling, but they all seem to originate with our pursuit of God, or lack thereof.

In addition to the pursuit of God, I also focus on a few landmines that cause us to retreat from our pursuit. I also included a chapter that will help pastors overcome many health challenges. *How we steward our physical health greatly affects our overall productivity and spiritual health.*

Ultimately, I hope to point out the most common tripwires before the explosions go off. But for those who have already stepped on a landmine and are seriously wounded, I'd like to offer hope to you as well: *Always remember that you plus God equals a majority!* He just needs one man fully surrendered to Him, or in many cases, re-surrendered.

The Two Are One

Pastors' wives also deal with tremendous pressure and are truly the unsung heroes of ministry. Like Cinderella, she often goes unnoticed and uncelebrated, yet she helps keep everything together. She is frequently judged by what she wears, how her children behave, and a dozen other things. She must always wear a smile regardless of how she truly feels. For this reason, I asked my wife, Morgan, to write a chapter specifically for leaders' wives: *I ALMOST QUIT, TOO.*

I can honestly say that without her, there would be no ministry. When God truly calls a man, He also calls his wife. The two are one, and wives need hope and encouragement as well.

My Brief Background

My journey back to God began around 1999. I was the typical prodigal son who repented and believed in Jesus when I was 12 years of age, but through a series of bad influences, including an unbelieving father, I remained lukewarm for over 17 years.

During that time, I made fun of those who worshipped God. Sure, I would pray from time to time and get emotional and lift my hands while watching the NFL, but in church, no way! At that time, I believed I was strong because I could bench-press over 400 pounds, drink a 12-pack of beer, and win most of the fights I was in. I didn't have control of my life — my life had control of me.

Sometime later, my life began falling apart, and I realized just how far I had drifted from the truth. By God's grace, I put my complete trust in Him. Joy, happiness, and peace filled my heart. Then came books, speaking engagements, and ultimately, a church.

God took a dyslexic nobody from a small town in Southern California with learning and speech problems who barely graduated high school with a 1.8 GPA, and filled him with the Holy Spirit. It was a very emotional day that I still remember decades later.

From there, I began to develop a deep hunger for theological topics. I devoured C.H. Spurgeon and D. Martyn Lloyd-Jones, and books on systematic theology — everyone from Wayne

Grudem to Norman Geisler and Charles Hodge to John MacArthur.

Because of the deep work of the Spirit in my life, I also gravitated towards books written about revivals in the 1700s and 1800s, as well as prayer and fasting resources from leaders such as Leonard Ravenhill, A.W. Tozer, and E.M. Bounds. I couldn't get enough.

I also quickly learned that there were different theological camps within Christianity. I understand division with those who do not embrace the essentials of the faith, but I had difficulty understanding *why* there was so much division over the non-essentials.

For this reason, I decided to balance my reading between people such as Jack Hayford and John MacArthur — both were located about an hour south of me, but were miles apart in some of their theological views.

In reading Charismatics and Calvinists, Pentecostals and Puritans, as well as countless biographies of leaders such as Martin Luther, John Calvin, John Knox, John Wesley, Robert Murray M'Cheyne, and D.L. Moody, and Puritans such as Thomas Goodwin, John Bunyan, John Owen, and Richard Baxter, I realized that it's *the truth* that unites us.

When great men of God disagree on the non-essentials, I try to hold my opinions loosely (note the word "try"). I want to remain teachable and humble throughout my pursuit of God, but at times, it can be challenging. Yes, I have strong feelings about some of the non-essentials, but I don't want to cause division in the Body of Christ when it's avoidable. **My pride loves to argue about theology, but the voice of humility must be louder.**

I'm well aware of the risk of writing a book like this when I'm still pastoring; the statistics are *not* on my side regarding pastors finishing well, but I'm hopeful because when God guides, He guards.

Our attitude and pursuit of God (or lack thereof) deeply affect those we lead. The landmines we step on not only hurt us but also those around us. In short, we set the spiritual temperature of our churches. I pray that this book inspires and uplifts pastors no matter where they are in their journey.

For more resources, visit ShaneIdleman.com and subscribe to my podcasts: *Idleman Unplugged & Pastors Unplugged.* I also put my *Top 10 Articles for Pastors* on my website and embedded them in this link for eBook readers.

Chapter One

Why I Almost Quit

"So teach us to number our days,
that we may gain a heart of wisdom"
(Psalm 90:12)

By 2024, I had reached a tipping point: I no longer wanted to pastor anymore, and I wasn't sure why. *Looking back, I don't believe that it had to do with stress as much as discouragement.*

It all started during the COVID-19 pandemic. As a church in Los Angeles County, the stress was overwhelming at times. First, there was the stress of the unknown and not knowing what to expect. Second was the stress of dealing with all the contradictory voices: Government authorities giving mixed messages, division among Christian leaders, and people in our own congregation arguing among themselves regarding everything from social distancing to the mRNA vaccine. The number of people leaving California was alarming, and don't get me started on the masks!

We decided to open our church just two months into the pandemic. We were also able to move to an outdoor stadium for Saturday night services in the summer, and that's when Los Angeles County tightened its grip. The stress resulted in everything from lost sleep and overeating to being rude to those who disagreed with our stance.

Undoubtedly, every pastor went through extreme turmoil during the pandemic. There was no precedent to help us make decisions. At times, I truly felt helpless, but praise God, He strengthened me through it, and we came out much stronger. Our confidence and faith soared, and we actually grew numerically and financially during this very challenging season. Fortunately, we held our course and stayed open, and the spiritual fruit was amazing.[2]

Adding to my discouragement was the death of my mom, who was an incredible spiritual encouragement. On September 22, 2020, I received a text from her that said she needed prayer because she wasn't feeling too well. That was the last text that I ever received from her. She passed away shortly after that from an aneurysm, and the hospital near Boise, Idaho, would not allow any visitors while she lay conscious in the emergency room, talking with others. She died a few minutes later while telling the doctors about us kids. The hospital would not let my sister and brother visit in her final moments. To say that I was furious is an understatement. I was ready to drive 12 hours and confront the administration, but I decided to sleep on it. God really healed my heart that night, and I decided not to make the drive. I was then given the daunting task of putting her entire memorial service together, including speaking at it. I could feel the stress taking its toll.

---

[2] *Stadium Revival Draws over 1,000 Worshipers in California*. Read here.

Now, fast-forward a few years, when other career options began to present themselves. A friend was adamant that I should run for governor of California, and a few others agreed. In my heart, I knew this wasn't my wheelhouse, but California was a mess. For the first time in my life, I was considering a different career path, as if running for governor would be less stressful and discouraging — yeah, right!

Then, I was encouraged to consider the potential of leading a large parachurch ministry in another state. Since I was still confused, disgruntled, and distant, I definitely thought about it.

As a third option, I considered moving to Idaho. My brother had moved there years ago and was doing extremely well. I was praying about asking to join him and start a few businesses and work together again like we had done in the past.

All of these options hit me at different stages of my journey. The point of sharing this is to demonstrate that the enemy often uses "good plans" to replace "God's plans." For a lengthy season, showing up on Sundays and Wednesdays to fulfill my duties was very challenging. **Pastoring was no longer a passion but an obligation.**

Wounded on the Battlefield

By this time in ministry, the relational pain was also reaching a crescendo. Only pastors know how it feels to pour into people for years and then have them turn on you — it can really wear on you — not to mention how many friends and co-laborers moved out of California. It was definitely a hard season.

Obviously, we have to take responsibility for some of the fallout we experience, but after working with thousands of people for many years and watching many pastors go through similar challenges, the bottom line is that tearing down pastors often makes people feel better. When we lovingly challenge someone about their attitude and behavior, instead of repenting, changing, and growing, most people make *us* the target of their anger.

It's beautiful when people work on their shortcomings together (including pastors); the relationship becomes even stronger as a result. *But I'm sad to report that's rarely the case — most people leave the church when they are lovingly confronted.* If we add to the mix the people who have a tendency to be judgmental about the worship, the flow of the service, and the sermon topics, as well as what you wear, how you lead, and any other thing they can find to complain about, it can really be depressing.

Health Can Aid Healing

Not only was pastoring wearing on me, but so was my health. Once I reached my 50s, there were definite hormonal shifts taking place, such as lower testosterone levels. I also experienced higher blood pressure, inflammation, muscle loss, and weight gain, along with other symptoms resembling prediabetes. I was developing what many experts are now calling "metabolic syndrome."

This was hard to swallow because I have an extensive background in health and fitness, but the bottom line was that weighing 220 lbs. at 6' 2" may have been permissible in my younger years, but not now. **I knew what to do; I was just having a hard time doing it.** Isn't that the case with so many of us?

An acquaintance of mine, Gary Brecka, said that 90% of people never sprint again after age 30. I set out to be part of the 10%, but instead, I severely pulled and possibly tore my hamstring, which set me back for the rest of the year. Additionally, my blood pressure was climbing, and I was out of energy. The downward spiral continued. *I appeared fit on the outside, but not on the inside.*

The Clock Was Ticking

I would wake up in the morning and not want to do anything. **The clock was ticking, but I wasn't changing.** I was still following my pattern over the last 25 years of waking up between 3 am and 4 am, listening to worship, and praying, but I felt like God was very distant and that I was simply going through the motions.

Ironically, I was doing well in my walk with the Lord in terms of my home life. My marriage and family were never stronger. The people I pastor, as well as our staff and volunteers, were wonderful. *So it wasn't the people — it was me.* I was growing weary, worn out, and exhausted.

In addition to having five kids at home, three of whom were teenagers, our church bought two radio stations in Los Angeles County in 2019, and I became the de facto manager, accountant, and marketer. If a transmitter wasn't down, the internet was, and if a cradlepoint wasn't out of order, our air conditioning units were. Even though I had taken a sabbatical a few years earlier, I couldn't figure out what was going on. I quickly learned that you can't thrive spiritually on yesterday's blessing.

One More Major Disappointment

After nearly 15 years of pastoring and 25 years in ministry, I was getting older and life was flying by — a true midlife crisis. But specifically, there was *one more* major disappointment that had a compounding effect. Our church is in a rural area, on the outskirts of the more populated area in Los Angeles County. After nearly fifteen years of praying for a large, centrally located building with plenty of space for kids, youth, and fellowship, I realized that my dream *might* not have been God's dream.

Some of my pastor friends were planting churches around my home in areas where I felt God had called me to. To say I was confused is an understatement! But of course, we can't share struggles like this with others, or they'll think we're prideful and self-focused. But that wasn't the case at all; I was simply responding to a deep inner calling that's been gnawing at me ever since we planted the church.

Fortunately, I wasn't jealous; I was just perplexed. I truly wanted other churches to thrive and lead people to Christ in my community. Did I miss God's will … something I'd been praying about for a long time? **But here I was, fifteen years later, with a dead dream.** If you've been there as well, you know exactly what I'm talking about.

I know all about faith and trusting in God even when we don't see the miracle, but it's definitely easier to *preach it* than it is to *live it*. I also reflected often on Mark 11:24, "Whatever things you ask when you pray, believe that you receive them, and you will have them." Despite all my "believing," I was not "receiving." The heavens were truly brass.

I was worn out and weary. I thought, "This dream location was a good idea, but maybe it wasn't God's idea." I chewed on that tension between His will and my will for years. But ultimately, I trusted Him and rested in His sovereignty. It was a process, but joy eventually followed. **His sovereignty truly was my sanity.**

God knows what's best, so I trusted Him completely. This brought peace where there once was turmoil.

I also had other ideas over the years, such as God calling me to speak to pastors and write more books, but I had zero motivation to write, let alone travel. All of this led to massive discouragement and ultimately, depression: *I almost quit!*

Pulling Out of the Nose Dive

Let me tell you up-front that the answers were not profound or deep, and I understand that there are pastors who are going through very difficult seasons, but I believe that what God brought me through can help many others (and even those who are not pastors).

In the following chapters, I will unpack key landmines that primarily focus on the topic of pursuing God. These landmines can derail and detour our destiny if we get off course. You must take them seriously. The good news is that many landmines have delayed triggers. The key is to jump off before the explosion occurs. In God's grace and mercy, He often gives us plenty of warning and plenty of time.

If you are currently standing on a landmine, or if the explosion has already taken place, take time now and repent while you have the chance. It will hurt, but the fruit of repentance far outweighs the fruit of exposure that will surely come (cf. Num. 32:23). A penitent person turns from sin. They accept full responsibility for their actions without blame, resentment, or bitterness. They seek forgiveness without conditions and stipulations. They take full responsibility for their actions. There can be no "buts" when repentance is genuine. "I am sorry. I was wrong. Please forgive me" are often (though not always) healing words and signs of true repentance. In my case, excuses were clouding my spiritual vision. Excuses need to stop in order for healing to occur, and this is where we must begin.

1st Step to Freedom:
Repentance, Seeking, and Thankfulness

First, despite how I *felt*, I prayed for strength and pressed into God even more. Perseverance is a key biblical principle that will produce godly fruit — period. Regardless of how I *felt*, I knew that if I sought Him, I would eventually find Him (Jer. 29:13). The *truth* was my anchor, not my *feelings*.

Christians should be the most joy-filled people on the planet, and I knew I had to repent for being disgruntled and discouraged. This vital step was key to my breakthrough. We know that God is everywhere, but there's something profound when we can literally sense His presence and power working in our lives — when we are spiritually energized and focused. Healing takes time, so I set my mind on the long haul, beginning with thankfulness.

I also prayed Psalm 90:12 on a consistent basis to teach me to prioritize my days in order to acquire wisdom. I asked God to teach me what I'm supposed to be learning through this trial so I can make better choices and prepare for the next step. As pastors, we too must ask for wisdom, and according to James 1:5, God will grant us that request as long as we don't doubt and complain during the process.

2nd Step to Freedom:
Renewed Focus on Physical Health and Discipline

Second, because I was consuming too much food throughout the day in an attempt to deal with my discouragement, I was also paying the price physically. I knew that I had to focus more on my physical health as well as self-discipline, because the physical often affects the spiritual.

Can you pray and seek God better with a headache, tight clothes, and a very sluggish and lethargic body? Of course not. What you put in the mouth [body] and the mind [soul] affects the spirit. For example, a person may say, "Please pray for my panic attacks, angry outbursts, and anxiety." We can do that, but they may want to consider if what they're eating and drinking is contributing to their anxiety. Again, the physical affects the spiritual.

For instance, once I minimized caffeine consumption, I eventually started to feel much better, even though the strong withdrawals initially added to my depression. It shows just how powerful caffeine is. I know that many pastors won't want to hear that, but it's the truth (moderation may be okay, but very few use it in moderation). I also began to consume less food and incorporated a smaller eating window. *I preached about other sins, but rarely touched on the sacred cow of gluttony.*

During this time, Proverbs 25:28 really jumped out to me: "A man without self-control is like a city broken into and left without walls." First Corinthians 9:25 reminded me that Christians are to exercise self-control. Although I've always been active, I had grown complacent, and it was time to up my game and become more active. I began to make phone calls while walking instead of while sitting at my desk. This simple change added a great deal of discipline to my life, which helped me feel better both physically and spiritually.

Proverbs 25:16 was my final motivation: "Eat only as much honey as you need." I ate because I *wanted* food, not because I *needed* it. For those of you who might be thinking this is not a big deal, I can assure you that it *is*. Because of the chemical changes that take place in the body, food works like a drug. Like most people, I used food to cope with life.

Eventually, my weight gain led to more health problems, which led to more discouragement. It was a vicious cycle. After talking to countless pastors, I know that this is a common struggle. I was fascinated to read about Christians throughout history who practiced moderation and fasting. **We must control our appetites rather than allow our appetites to control us.**

It's incredible how much overconsumption and gluttony can weigh us down spiritually. My heart breaks for pastors who are unhealthy. I know that they would feel so much better if they lost weight and took better care of their bodies: They would be much more productive, have better energy, and enjoy better moods. *There is no question in my mind that they would be better leaders.*

The *type* of food we consume also plays a significant role in our mental health. About 90% of serotonin is created in the gut; therefore, having a healthy gut microbiome is key to overall health. Eating God-given food in moderation while being much more active is a must — it all works together. *How could I consistently give in to my appetite and still seek the heart of God? I don't think it's possible.*

3rd Step to Freedom:
Content with My Calling

Third, I began to pray and really believe these words: "Lord, if this is all you have for me, You know what's best. Please forgive me for being disgruntled. You have given me a wonderful church and an incredible family. I am truly blessed. If my calling is to pastor this community church tucked back in the rolling hills of Leona Valley, I will do it with joy and fervency."

This was a huge breakthrough. Many pastors rate success by numbers and not by faithfulness. That might work for corporate America, but not for God's corporation. Whether you're called to lead 25 or 25,000, God knows what's best. Trust Him and surrender to His will.

The irony is that we have a large congregation in a small town and my sermons reach tens of thousands of people each day on many different radio outlets from San Diego to Los Angeles and from Dallas to New York. I was content; I didn't want more exposure or followers because the larger you are, the more issues you have to deal with.

Business leader Peter Drucker has pointed out that two of the most difficult jobs in the world are to be president of the United States and to be a leader of a megachurch. So it wasn't about the numbers; it was about how I was *feeling* and wondering if I missed God's will. There's that dreaded word again — *feelings*. Don't trust them, especially before making a major decision!

Once I rested in God's sovereignty and accepted where He wanted me, joy followed. That decision opened the door for more opportunity and influence because of repentance. I wasn't perfect, but I was re-focused and re-energized: "Lord, wherever You want to place me is fine with me," was my daily prayer.

Luke 16:10 reminds us that when we are faithful in the little things, God may give us more. Wanting to bypass the process of growth reveals *a lot* about a leader's motives. *Why are they leading? Is it to build an extensive ministry, or is it to build up people?*

Many pastors quit because they feel they are not being "used." Let me reassure you that you are being used — that's not the problem. The problem, many times, is that you are not being recognized, esteemed, or promoted. God desires humility and servitude, not arrogance and pride. Meekness and boastfulness *cannot* co-exist.

Unfortunately, being disgruntled is the catalyst for resentment and bitterness. And sadly, this is often why many pastors pull down other leaders and other churches — they are not happy with their own situation.

We will not be disappointed if we understand that God desires us to have the heart of a servant. "Those who follow Christ must not expect great or high things in this world" (Matthew Henry). "Expect" is the key word. God may promote a person for His glory, but we should never "expect" this. **Finding peace and satisfaction, no matter where God places you, is the key to avoiding most landmines.**

4th Step to Freedom:
Show Up Regardless of "Feelings"

Fourth, even though I didn't "feel" like it, I showed up to preach, minister, and lead. When we allow God's love to flow through us, it not only helps others but it renews our spiritual life — it becomes life-giving to us as well as to them.

During this difficult time, I heard a pastor in an interview say, "If you can see the light in the darkness, you can handle the sunlight of destiny." He also added: "Can you honor people who don't honor you and keep focusing on the dream in the middle of the nightmare?"[3] His words cut deep. I learned a very

---

[3] Although I can no longer find the interview, I believe that it was Dale Mast.

important principle: **Don't become frustrated, become fervent.** Extended prayer and deep fasting were game-changers for me. We must fervently seek the Lord and strengthen ourselves in Him. There is no Plan B.

Victory's Light Shines in Darkness

You often hear the saying, "It didn't happen overnight." This is because God's refining work often takes time. Jeremiah 29:13 was an enormous encouragement to me during this time: "And you will seek Me and find Me, when you search for Me with all your heart." To *seek* in this context means to "find what is missing."

Imagine losing your child in a crowded mall. How would you spend your time? Where would your energy be focused? Now, compare this with seeking God. In the same way that you would devote all your time, energy, and focus to find your lost child, you must make your pursuit of God your priority.

Like the children of Israel during the Exodus, I was stuck in neutral because I was disgruntled. To add more to the emotional mix, the enemy was also shooting fiery darts into my mind: "Who are you? You're a nobody. You didn't even go to seminary. Look at your past!"

Early in my ministry, the pastor of a church in my area told his members that we were not a real church because I didn't attend seminary. Never mind the countless hours I spent buried in God's Word, commentaries, biographies, and numerous books on systematic theology; this particular pastor was hell-bent on tearing me down. And that's just one example of many. Although there are still battles, the joy eventually returned when I spent time truly seeking God. I felt the Spirit awaken me. Looking back, I see that I had to go through this dark season to test my faith — would I keep seeking Him? Would I help others pull out of the same pit that I was once in? My preaching also took on a new dimension. People commented, "There is something different about you." I knew the answer, but I wasn't yet ready to share my journey.[4]

Soon after this time, I received requests to speak at pastors' conferences. God was clearly confirming what I was sensing. Once we truly say, "Not my will but Your will be done," there is often joy because the load is lifted. **So much of our pressure in ministry comes from our dreams "about" ministry — what "I" want to do instead of what "God" wants me to do.**

Years ago, I remember Pastor Steve Schell talking about the day his depression lifted. He was in a buffet line talking to a couple who were overflowing with joy, even though the husband led a very small church. Pastor Schell realized that his success was tied to numbers, not faithfulness. Once he repented, God renewed his passion, and the depression vanished. How about you? Are you thankful no matter where you're serving?

The Road is Still Rough

Keep in mind that I still deal with difficult seasons; they are part of our fallen nature, but now they are an occasional struggle rather than a constant challenge. *The road is still rough, but at least my feet are secure.*

I realize this is not the case for everyone and that some pastors have been stuck for years with no relief in sight. In these cases, I encourage them to take their frustration to the Lord through

---

[4] Ebook readers can click here to hear a sermon that happened right after this time, or search for, *Pursuit Was Their Passion,* on our platforms dated 3/30/25.

prayer and fasting and see how He directs them. Sometimes a thorn in our flesh remains to keep us humble, but at other times, deep repentance may need to take place before the chains of discouragement can be broken.

Finally, there could be a demonic stronghold that needs to be dealt with, a chemical imbalance that needs attention, or health changes that need to occur. Only God truly knows. Even the great preacher Charles Spurgeon struggled with depression. **Follow his example and focus on the eternal, not on the temporal.**

Chapter Two: Passion

The Shepherds Have Become Dull-hearted

"Oh, that You would rend the heavens!"
(Isaiah 64:1)

In David Ravenhill's book, *Surviving the Anointing*, he makes a powerful statement that very few people survive the anointing. They grow dull-hearted, and instead of humbling themselves and repenting, pride gains a foothold and causes them to drift into spiritual decline.

But how does a pastor become dull-hearted? 1) They never were passionate about God to begin with, or 2) they failed to keep the fire burning by seeking God, praying, obeying, and staying broken, humble, and contrite. He will "revive the spirit of the humble" (Isa. 57:15). *Staying spiritually sharp is directly related to spiritual disciplines done with the right heart.*

Are You Too Busy to Drink?

I once shared with our congregation that one of the most difficult challenges associated with pastoring is not sermon preparation or taxing appointments, but witnessing the tragic results of spiritual dehydration — people dying spiritually with living water easily within reach. But equally alarming is the number of pastors and leaders who are spiritually dehydrated. I've been there myself.

Sadly, we become too busy and self-absorbed to drink deeply from the well of the living water that Christ spoke of (Jh. 7:38). This lack of fervency is reflected in the short poem by Wilbur Reese:

> "I would like to buy three dollars' worth of God, please. Not enough to explode my soul or disturb my sleep, but just enough to equal a cup of warm milk, or a snooze in the sunshine ... I want ecstasy, not transformation. I want the warmth of the womb, not a new birth. I want a pound of the eternal in a paper sack. I would like to buy three pounds of God, please."

The excuses as to why we don't seek God more fervently than we do are broad, but the solution is narrow: "Whoever drinks the water I give him will never thirst" (Jh. 4:14). Because of compromise, pride, busyness, and so on, very few leaders are truly hungry and thirsty for God. They either enjoy being somewhat worldly or they proudly wear the Modern-day Pharisee badge and lean toward legalism. Either extreme will quench the fire of the Spirit: "For the shepherds have become dull-hearted, and have not sought the Lord ... " (Jer. 10:21).

On this point, Gene Easley's words cut deep: "We'll have Church when God comes, but not until then. All of our religious activities mean nothing without His hallowed presence." Easley concludes, "The dilemma that brings us shame is that we have learned how to have church as usual whether He is here or not. The week is full of activities — we know how to keep the programs going. We know how to play our part. The machinery continues to operate, but the mountains won't move until He comes."[5]

Our prayer must be: "Oh God, fill us again and begin in me!"

You Have as Much of God as You Want

An illustration I once read in an old commentary described a king who told all his subjects that on a given day, the fountain in the center of the city would flow with expensive juices and oils, and that everyone was free to bring their vessels and carry away as much as they liked. The man who brought a small glass got a glassful; the man who brought a gallon pitcher received even more. *In short, we have as much of God as we want — as much as we pursue.*

Most pastors will *say* they are pursuing God, but *saying* is a lot easier than *doing*. Although most of us quote, "Blessed are those who hunger and thirst for righteousness, for they shall be filled," many have lost their way.

Paul said that He wants to know Christ in the power of His resurrection and in the fellowship of His suffering (Php. 3:10). King David cried out, "One thing I have asked from the Lord, that I shall seek: That I may dwell in the house of the Lord all the days of my life" (Ps. 27:4). Hungering and thirsting for God is an all-consuming pursuit that drives every aspect of life.

---

[5] *Fire Upon the Altar* by Gene Easley © 1994 pg. 101.

As important as our work in the ministry is, seeking God must be our primary passion. Study and sermon preparation, although vastly important, don't necessarily produce hunger if our heart is not right. **The priority of prayer, the preeminence of worship, and the power of the Word are the only things that can get us back on track.** The inflow into our heart affects what outflows to the people. If there's a disconnect with God, the problem is not on His end, but on ours.

Sadly, many have lost their spiritual hunger and their passion for pursuing God and have become gruff and grumpy, or lazy and lukewarm. We must repent of apathy to experience God's fire again. We have as much of God as we want.

Wrong Pursuits Dull the Blade

Pursuing the wrong things, even *good* things if they come before God, can cost a great deal. The passion and the priority of seeking God are what keeps it all together, and what keeps *us* together. Not denominational goals and larger ministries — not the opinions of men nor worldly pursuits — but the pursuit of God. He is our ONLY source of spiritual life and wholeness. *"Beware, if God is not first in His glory, our own glory will be our downfall" (Josiah Shute).*

If you survey the lives of fallen leaders, you'll find that they became dull-hearted because they pursued the wrong things and went off course. This dangerous landmine of losing our passion is often hidden in the grass of excuses. As I wrote in the introduction, our attitude and passion for God (or lack thereof) deeply affect those who sit under our ministry. **We set the spiritual temperature of our churches.** If we are negative and grumpy, that tone will be set. In contrast, if we're weak and liberal, we will steer our churches in that direction as well.

One of the ways that we encourage our congregation to pursue God and lead by example is by opening each Sunday at 6 a.m. with worship on the sound system until our 7:30 a.m. prayer meeting, followed by the 8:30 a.m. and 11 a.m. services. When we rush through or shorten our services, we often miss the deeper work of the Spirit. I'm not saying this is the case for everyone — I realize that some churches need shorter services, especially those with parking issues, etc. **But I've found that seeking God is never convenient or quick.**

He Pours In So We Can Pour Out

I have found that after many years of pastoring, it can become challenging to come up with fresh sermons. But the more time I spend with God, the more He pours into me. This is why most books on pastoring encourage pastors not to use sermon preparation as their devotional time. *To generate passion, we often need to put down the pen. The key to spiritual health is not found on the keyboard but in keeping close to the Savior.*

We all know about David strengthening himself in the Lord in the midst of a very challenging situation (see 1 Sam. 30:6). Why is it important for us to also "strengthen ourselves in the Lord"? *Because we can't take others where we ourselves have never been.* To strengthen yourself begins with a decision to seek God no matter the cost. That's motivation, but you also need discipline. Motivation makes the commitment, but discipline fulfills it. Motivation will only take you as far as discipline will carry you. But be encouraged: The more you apply discipline, the more motivation you will generate. As the Word says, "Blessed are those who hunger and thirst" (Mat. 5:6). It's important to work up the motivation … the thirst, but it's just as important to pursue God via discipline.

Pray, "Lord, let the rivers of Living Water flow in and out of me again," and desire the heart found in Psalm 84:2, "My soul longs, yes, even faints for the courts of the Lord. My heart and my flesh cry out for the living God." But also pray for the discipline to pursue the Living Water. *If you're worried about being labeled as too extreme or overzealous, realize that you will be labeled regardless, so you might as well let God label you as a man after His own heart.*

I've heard it said that the greatest hindrance to drawing near to God is our satisfaction without Him. It's not comfortable nor convenient to truly seek God. Unction is the dire need in the pulpit today, but this only comes through a man on fire for God. Leonard Ravenhill once said to a group of pastors, "Get unction, or get out of the pulpit." The point of his statement was to spur them on to pursue a deeper walk with God — a deeper passion.

Developing passion is ultimately about dependency: I desperately need God; He is my only hope: "Blessed are the beggars" (Mat. 5:3). A.W. Tozer was right in his counsel: "My recommendation for the church today is to call a moratorium on all activity and focus on coming into worship until the fire descends and engulfs us in the sacredness of His presence!" *A choice must be made to seek Him or to sulk; to fan the flames of desire or to blow them out.* **The place of sorrow must become a place of surrender.** You can prepare a good sermon, but lack a prepared heart. God pours in so you can pour out.

The Bill for Regret

I heard a story some time ago that made me laugh out loud, and it definitely applies here. A boy named Little Johnny got his hand stuck in a very expensive vase that had been passed down from his grandparents. His mom became upset when she couldn't pull out his little hand, so she called the fire department. They tried as well, but to no avail. Finally, the dad arrived home and was forced to get a hammer from the garage.

Just before hitting the expensive and precious vase, Little Johnny asked, "Would it help if I let go of the penny?" There was a gasp followed by a loud "Yes!" We laugh, but isn't that so true with us in regard to our pursuits and desires? We must surrender in order to build passion. **If you think the price of full surrender is too expensive, wait until you get the bill for regret!**

His Presence — Our Pursuit

Although God is everywhere, what we call omnipresent, there is a marked difference between a believer who is dry spiritually and dead inside, in contrast to one who is full of passion, desire, and fire. The corridors of church history are filled with stories of Christians being spiritually dead but then coming alive. What changed? What happened?

In short, they began to pursue God like never before. They experienced a fresh filling of the Spirit. Whether you want to call it a baptism, unction, or anointing, you'd better have it. To achieve it, we must abandon our idols, repent of lukewarmness, and truly seek God — His presence must be our pursuit. When you seek God, you will find Him (Jer. 29:13).

The Word of God that comes from your lips must flow from the deep work that God is doing in your heart. **Stagnation always leads to stale sermons.** We must take up our cross again. Yes, it's rugged, tough, sharp, and inconvenient, but it's the only way to truly pursue Him. In darkness, you can still praise Him, in depression, you can still seek Him, and in fear, you can still follow Him. He is the only anchor for our soul; the Rock of our salvation. Pursue Him with fervency!

Pursuit Produces Boldness

It's no surprise that passionate Spirit-filled bold preaching is in decline — just look at the average sermon preached each week. A report from the *American Worldview Inventory 2022* showed that just 37% of Christian pastors have a biblical worldview. Barna noted, "Our survey demonstrates that large numbers of pastors have abandoned even the most basic and hallowed biblical teachings for ideas that now permeate our culture."

The spiritual decline in America is largely due to the spiritual decline in pastors. In addition to encouraging and uplifting others, those who are called to preach should also confront compromise, condemn moral digression, and powerfully denounce sin in the hope of reconciling man to God. The world despises them because they challenge the sin they enjoy. Trying to please a Christ-rejecting world is an exercise in futility.

Although ruffling feathers is not our goal, we will step on toes from time to time when we pursue God and proclaim His truth. This can't always be avoided, nor should it be. We need more men like the Old Testament prophet Micaiah, who said, "As surely as the Lord lives, I will speak whatever the Lord tells me" (1 Kgs. 22:14).

God honors and emboldens the preacher who speaks the truth. Boldness is a byproduct of passionately pursuing God. **If you're too worried about the opinions of men, you will become a motivational speaker rather than an anointed leader** (cf. Luk. 16:15). Speaking the heart of God flows from a reservoir of brokenness and time spent pursuing Him. How are you doing in this area? Is the absolute truth of God's Word the foundation of your preaching as well as your pursuit?

The Fruit of Spiritual Barrenness

When our pursuit of God fades, we lack the fire of the Spirit and the thundering of truth. Sadly, many replace them with gimmicks and silly illustrations. Granted, I'm all for sermon illustrations if they are *truly* prompted by God and not being used to cover the lack of anointing on our preaching.

Instead of spending time with God as broken, humble messengers needing a touch from Him, some pastors spend time filling their minds with the world. Using gimmicks for sermon illustrations, such as kicking a Bible, swallowing a sword, spitting in a person's face, taking a bath, and getting a haircut on stage, is often a byproduct of spiritual barrenness. They've lost their passion for God.

The Desperate Need Today

The word "revival" is very popular right now, but it also carries some negative connotations. When I use that word, I'm talking about a legitimate downpour of God's Spirit that transforms the environment.[6]

So why aren't we seeing revival in a fuller measure? In Duncan Campbell's book, *The Price and Power of Revival,* he made the following statement:

> "One of the main secrets of success in the early Church lay in the fact that the early believers believed in unction from on high and not entertainment from men. How did the early Church get the people? By publicity projects ... by posters, by parades, by pictures? No! The people were

---

[6] My interview with CBN News regarding revival can be viewed here.

arrested and drawn together and brought into vital relationship with God, not by sounds from men, but by sounds from heaven ... Unction is the dire and desperate need of the ministry today."

We must humble ourselves and *remove compromise* if we are to experience the power of the Spirit working in our lives. In Old Testament Israel, thousands still sacrificed to God on the high places even though it was forbidden. "At least we're sacrificing to God," they thought. Whether for convenience or because of compromise, God's people began to justify the use of pagan locations and altars to offer to God. God's heart must have broken each time the Bible records: "But the high places were not removed" (1 Kgs. 15:14).

Like Israel, are there areas in our lives where we're allowing compromise to seep in? As a famous poem reminds us:

"All the water in the world,
However hard it tried,
Could never sink the smallest ship
Unless it gets inside.
And all the evil in the world,
The blackest kind of sin,
Can never hurt you in the least
Unless you let it in."

Kill Compromise Before It Kills You

Be hopeful: If your passion has faded because of compromise, you can change that right now! In the same way that physical cancer is often reversed when the fuel source is removed or the rogue cells killed, spiritual cancer can also be reversed if we remove sin and kill its source.

What places of compromise do you need to repent of? What areas of ungodly influence do you need to let go of? What attitudes need adjustment? We must return to the prayer closet and get back to the basics of prayer, fasting, and humility. *We are waiting on God, but could it be that He is waiting on us?*

We Can't "Work It Up"

Now that you're encouraged, let me offer a warning: Some mistakenly believe that spiritual intensity is measured by volume — that louder preaching and vocal prayers automatically get God's attention. *You may work the people up, but you won't bring down the Spirit.* Some of the most powerful sermons and prayers I've ever heard were quiet yet very deep and heartfelt.

Additionally, a circus environment devoid of scriptural grounding doesn't elevate the Spirit — it stifles it. The misguided notion that "if it's odd, it must be God" is dangerous. Scripture warns us explicitly that we should not grieve or quench the Spirit, and yes, this can apply to weird behavior and not stewarding the environment correctly. (cf. Eph. 4:30; 1 Thess. 5:1.)

I know I'm preaching to the choir, but it's a good reminder that we pastors can also extinguish God's fire in our midst by trying to whip up a Holy Spirit pep rally. We can't generate it — God has to bring it down!

Experience Doesn't Validate Truth

On the flip side, many wrongly assume that those who passionately pursue God are seeking experiences and feelings over Christ. What a mischaracterization of those who genuinely desire more of God. We seek Christ wholeheartedly because of our passion for Him.

Be careful that pride isn't clogging the outpouring of the Spirit in your life, or you'll be very critical of others. **As the old saints used to say: "Straight as a gun barrel theologically, but just as empty."** We should never interpret Scripture based on our experiences, but we can definitely validate our experiences based on Scripture. Many have experienced the Holy Spirit as described in the Book of Acts, and these encounters align with Scripture.

God gave us feelings, so wouldn't it be ideal to experience His presence from time to time? The power of the Holy Spirit is like dynamite that ignites a hunger for God so intense that every aspect of life is changed. Many see people acting weird, and they don't want anything to do with the Holy Spirit. *I get it, but I'm not going to let my relationship with God rise and fall on the actions of others.* In the same way, I'm not going to reject the Bible just because cults use it.

Do You *Truly* Want Revival?

The need to address revival and the vital role of the Holy Spirit remains as relevant today as it has throughout church history, and it is directly related to this chapter on passionately pursuing God. When we put God in a box, a spiritual awakening within us may never occur. We must humble ourselves, repent of childlike behavior, begin to fear God again, and be open to going deeper. *In short, a revival of the spiritual condition of His people is the only thing that will reinstall joy and hope.*

Many do not truly want to be revived because of the fear of what it may involve. Years ago, I prayed, "Lord, bring revival to the churches" — I was not ready for what followed. I felt impressed with these words:

"You don't want revival — it will ruin your schedule, your dignity, your image, and your reputation as a person who is 'well balanced.' Men will weep throughout the congregation. Women will wail because of the travail of their own souls. Young adults will cry like children at the magnitude of their sin. With the strength of My presence, the worship team will cease playing. Time will seem to stand still. You won't be able to preach because of the emotions flooding your own soul. You'll struggle to find words, but only find tears. Even the most dignified and reserved among you will be broken and humbled as little children. The proud and self-righteous will not be able to stand in My presence. The doubter and unbeliever will either run for fear or fall on their knees and worship Me — there can be no middle ground. The church will never be the same again."

Do you truly want revival? This is America's only hope. Are you willing to pay the price? There is a cost, and that cost is intimacy. We are reminded that God is merciful and slow to anger, but we must stop confusing His patience with His approval and begin pursuing Him again with all of our heart (Mat. 22:37).

Again, we are waiting on God, but could it be that He is waiting on us?

Special Note: Ironically, as I was inserting this into the book, God moved in a powerful way the following day at our first service on March 30th, 2025, and then again at the second service on April 6th. Two days that we will never forget. Links in the footnote.[7]

---

[7] Hear the sermon here, or search for, *Pursuit Was Their Passion* by Shane Idleman on YouTube, Rumble, etc. as well as *Pastor Explains the Revival Happening In SoCal* here.

Winning the War Within

"He acts for the one who waits for Him"
(Isaiah 64:4)

In a riveting blog from 2014 entitled, *Google Executive's Tragic Death Sends Somber Warning*, Dan Delzell wrote the following:

"How do you go from being a devoted father of five and a successful Silicon Valley executive, into a 51-year-old man convulsing from a fatal dose of heroin on your 50-foot yacht, with a prostitute walking over your dying body to take a final sip of wine before leaving you to die?" He then asked, "How do tragedies like this take place?" They occur when we consistently lose the battle within.

Galatians 5:17 says that the Spirit gives us desires that are opposite to what our sinful nature desires, and that these two influences are constantly fighting against each other. As a result, whether it's internal struggles, the pull toward laziness, or the desire to pursue worldly entertainment, our choices are rarely free from this conflict. *To finish well, we must choose spiritual life over spiritual death.*

John Owen wisely said, "Grace changes the nature of man, but nothing changes the nature of sin." In other words, our sinful nature and our new nature in Christ are constantly at war, and the pressure will never stop on this side of heaven. But be encouraged: The fact that there is a fight confirms the value of our commitment.

One Step at a Time

The enemy rarely pushes us off the cliff, so to speak. We're often led down one step at a time, one compromise at a time, one wrong choice at a time, until we eventually abandon our pursuit of God. For example, the enemy doesn't show a pastor the pain and anguish and the years of regret that adultery brings. If the whole story was known beforehand, different choices might have been made. **We're often not shown the pain that sin brings; rather, we're enticed by the temporary pleasure.**

The source of our strength comes from the food that we choose. What we feed grows, and what grows becomes the dominating force within our lives. Sin never stands still — it either grows or withers depending on whether you feed or starve it. In all cases when pastors fall, they lose their passion for God and back away from pursuing Him. *In my experience, no leader who was wholeheartedly pursuing God has ever succumbed to repeated, unrepentant moral failure.*

When a Pastor Goes to the Altar

Many churches encourage their congregations to commit or recommit their lives to God and suggest coming to the altar. It's not a biblical mandate, but it's an important suggestion. It can be very freeing when a person steps out and demonstrates their desperation for God, especially when pastors do this, but I have found that many pastors have lost their way to the altar. Whether or not you go to a physical altar is not the issue; the issue is the heart. Many think it's beneath them to humble themselves and admit their dependence on God. *In order for the Word of God to come alive in the hearts of others, it first must come alive in your own heart.*

The altar dethrones the idols we're currently bowing to, such as laziness, worldly pursuits, pride, education, etc. I know of pastors who would never go to the altar in the presence of the people they lead because they think it's beneath them. After all, what would people think? Sadly, the very thing they need is the very thing they are running from. *If you're a leader, why not lead them to the altar?* Why not demonstrate humility and brokenness and stop acting like you have it all together? A perfect marriage, perfect children, and a perfect life: it's a facade. *We all struggle.*

The altar is a place of brokenness that brings wholeness, a place of death that gives life, and a place of surrender that offers freedom. **God has called us to be shepherds to the shattered, rebuilders of the broken, and a place of worship for the wounded.** We don't stand above them; we serve alongside them to lift them up. Think how valuable your calling must be if the devil goes after it. The only way to guard it is to win the battle within. A church is only as healthy as its leaders. We must lead the way.

If you're caught in worldliness and have become lukewarm, or if pride and callousness have crept in, repent and ask God to revive the fire in your heart. Also, you must make choices that encourage a fresh filling rather than choices that quench the fire within. I've counseled many people who pray for a renewed passion for God, but won't give up what's grieving Him. They pray, "Lord, please take away this lust," but they won't confess to their wife that they need prayer, or set up accountability, or do anything else to quench sin. **A surefire way to weaken your pursuit of God is to strengthen your pursuit of sin.**

Darkness Should Not Entertain Us

What is the main culprit for extinguishing our pursuit of God? A.W. Tozer reminds us, "Who we are all week is who we will be when we step to the pulpit." The problem isn't Sunday; it's Monday and onward.

Ironically, as I was writing this, a prominent evangelical posted on X a statement that seemed to support Taylor Swift's lyrics. I'm not here to bash Taylor; she needs our prayers. But why would any leader promote this? Likely, it's because they've lost their passion for the pursuit of God. What we watch and listen to affects the heart; it's impossible to separate the two. **What goes into the heart ultimately comes out in actions.** The Scriptures are crystal clear on the entertainment issue; there's really no debate!

Philippians 4:8 says to fix our thoughts on what is true and honorable and right, and to think about things that are pure and lovely and admirable and worthy of praise. When darkness entertains us, it also influences us and dampens our fire for God. What you go to bed watching will determine your spiritual hunger (or lack thereof) in the morning.

Evil Never Reverses Course

Do we really believe that our flesh will simply reverse course? No, it will only get worse unless we apply spiritual disciplines to our lives. Puritan Thomas Tuke once wrote, "Like Jael to Sisera,

48

the world lulls its lovers to sleep with comforts, only to drive a nail through their temples." To avoid being lulled to sleep, we must cry out like Isaiah, "Oh God, would you rip heaven open and come down?" (cf. Isa. 64:1). Desperation and determination must fuel your pursuit. We must wait on God and seek Him like never before because "He acts for the one who waits for Him" (Isa. 64:4).

This type of waiting expects something to happen and waits patiently for it. When we wait, anger doesn't influence us, impatience doesn't drive us, and impulse doesn't derail us. The disciples tarried in the upper room until heaven opened and the Spirit came down. That experience forever changed them. They were always hungry for more of God. He was their all-consuming passion. They held on and never let go!

Answer the Call Today Without Delay

It has been estimated that only one out of every ten people entering the ministry today in their twenties will still be in it at age 65. **When devotion fades, sin betrays, and, as we all know, sin fascinates before it assassinates.** It's time to break up our fallow ground and seek the Lord while He still may be found (Hos. 10:12). *We provide the sacrifice; He provides the fire.*

We are undoubtedly familiar with the reminder in First Peter 5:8 that our "adversary the devil walks about like a roaring lion, seeking whom he may devour." But the Bible promises safety: "The eyes of the Lord run to and fro throughout the whole earth, to show Himself strong on behalf of those whose heart is loyal to Him" (2 Chr. 16:9). Will He find you seeking after Him, or running in the other direction?

There is nothing more painful than witnessing a leader running from God. Return to Him today and experience the joy of renewing your mind. Jesus promises relief to those who are exhausted: "Come to Me, all you who labor and are heavy laden, and I will give you rest" (Mat. 11:28). His call is to the fearful: "The peace of God, which surpasses all understanding, will guard your hearts and minds through Christ Jesus" (Php. 4:7). And His call is to the barren: "He who believes in Me, as the Scripture has said, out of his heart will flow rivers of living water" (Joh. 7:38).

Even if you're not where you'd like to be, God's love and mercy continually calls you back to Him. Don't extinguish the flames of revival; let them burn deeply in your soul. If we can quench the Spirit, we can be refueled; if we can grieve Him, we can once again have joy. *But we must feed our minds with things that strengthen our pursuit rather than hinder it.*

Practical Steps that Have Helped Me

Hopefully by now, your fire for God has been rekindled. Here are a few staples that will keep the fire ablaze and help you win the battle within. What I'm sharing is nothing new, but our *passion* for spiritual disciplines often needs to be refreshed. We don't necessarily need a list of priorities (although that can be helpful) — we need to prioritize biblical disciplines, and the rest often falls into place.

Although a fluctuating schedule can make some leaders lazy, the other extreme is often true, and we become too busy. As a result, our priorities become misaligned. Ironically, as I'm writing this chapter, a friend of mine who pastors a small church in our area told me he can't take any days off because his phone is continually ringing and there are constant needs. I get it. But that's not healthy. If you are like the pastor I just mentioned, perhaps you need to delegate some of your duties to other trustworthy people. *To be a better pastor, you must be a better balancer.*

1. Make prayer a priority above everything else. Men would live better if they prayed better and weren't in such a hurry. Whatever hurts our praying must be removed or minimized. Put your phone on airplane mode and don't constantly check emails or messages. Instead, keep a notepad next to you and write down your thoughts as they come, such as "I need to email this person" or "I need to look this up online." Don't do the tasks that come to your mind as soon as they occur, or they'll pull you away from intimacy with God. I'm not perfect in this area, but I try to do it each day. "In prayer it is better to have a heart without words than words without a heart" (John Bunyan).

Martin Luther famously said, "If I fail to spend two hours in prayer each morning, the devil gets the victory through the day. I have so much business, I cannot go without spending three hours daily in prayer." He added, "I have so much to do that I shall spend the first three hours in prayer."

Many say they don't have that much time to pray, but you'd be amazed at how much more time you could capture by prioritizing your day and going to bed earlier. The men who do the most for God are always men of prayer. "Preaching, in one sense, merely discharges the firearm that God has loaded in the silent place" (Calvin Miller).

E.M. Bounds reminds us: "The men who have done the most for God in this world have been early on their knees. He who fritters away the early morning, its opportunity and freshness, in other pursuits than seeking God will make poor headway seeking Him the rest of the day. If God is not first in our thoughts and efforts in the morning, He will be in the last place the remainder of the day." I can attest to the truth in this quote.

2. Schedule to read God's Word and meditate when you're fresh and not distracted. Have a systematic reading plan, such as 30 minutes a day. This helps settle my heart and points me in the right direction. If you encounter inspiring information for this week's sermon, note the thought down, but keep reading for your own edification. Note theological questions as well and seek to answer them later in the day. I can't tell you how many times I stopped reading to work on my sermon or to do a Greek or Hebrew word study, and it took me away from meditating on God's Word. As they say, *"Fill your mind with God's Word and you'll have no room for Satan's lies."*

3. End with prayer and ask for help to apply what you learned. Read a devotional such as "My Utmost For His Highest," and work on your sermon. Or, if you're a late-nighter, do the sermon work later. But always try to pray, worship, and meditate on God's Word before the day starts: "You can do more than pray after you have prayed; but you can never do more than pray until you have prayed" (A.J. Gordon).

4. Repeat this process in the evening when possible. *Remember, what you put into your mind in the PM is what you'll wake up with in the AM.* In other words, if you consume spiritual food in the evening, you will wake up desiring more of God in the morning. If we fill our minds with junk food, spiritually speaking, we'll wake up lethargic for the things of God.

5. Make sure to take time to build your marriage and your relationship with your children and/or grandchildren. Although the needs of your ministry may occasionally take you away from them, it should be the exception, not the rule. *You're only as healthy as your family is.* Your pursuit of God must be your main priority, followed by your marriage, then your role as a father, and then the ministry. Sometimes they overlap, but that shouldn't be the norm.

6. Consider fasting often; not out of obligation, but desperation: "You have not sought the Lord with 'your whole heart,' until you have tried a protracted season of prayer and fasting" (Gordon Cove). Cove continues: "In many cases where fastings have been added to the prayers, along with deep consecration and heart-searching before God, the answer has miraculously come to hand. When coupled to fasting, the prayer-power is greatly amplified." Also, don't forget that fasting has a powerful effect on the flesh that helps to overcome sin.

Here is how winning the battle in the mind plays out with all these points: During worship, the heart begins to soften as God draws your heart toward His. Repentance, if warranted, takes place and renews our passion for the truth. Reading the Word reinforces, educates, and opens our eyes to His will. Answering questions that we have builds faith (apologetics), and devotional reading sparks a deeper walk and hunger for God. *It's really about producing godly fruit, more than going through the motions of spiritual disciplines (Mat. 7:16-20).*

If you're looking for resources that go into more detail, exceptional books have been written specifically on the topic of godly disciplines, such as *Disciplines of a Godly Man* by R. Kent Hughes, as well as Albert N. Martin's insightful book, *The Man of God.*

What If I Fall?

In closing, I'd like to end with a letter I wrote to myself when we planted the church. I've never shared it before other than with a few people. When it comes to winning the battle within, we must consider where our choices will lead. Will they lead to shame and life-long embarrassment, or will they lead to joy because we finished well?

Although sin may be hidden for a season, eventually it becomes too big to hide: "When God is absent from ruling one's passions and controlling corrupt affections, only fire remains, and it is a fire that can quickly consume a household" (Josiah Shute).

"If I fall: My wife, kids, and countless others will lose respect for me and the ministry. It will hinder the gospel while unbelievers mock and scorn me until the day I die. The years of hard work in the ministry will crumble; a lifetime to build but only seconds to destroy. The kids and countless others may begin to doubt God as they struggle with disappointment and discouragement. My children will live the rest of their lives knowing that their dad failed, that he didn't finish well — he didn't practice what he preached. Instead of rejoicing over what God did through me, they (along with their children) will weep silently: *"Oh, how the mighty have fallen."*

This path of pain may open the door to addiction and suicidal harassment from the enemy. My relationship with my family may be fractured forever on this side of heaven — the pain will never be forgotten. The marriage, if it survives at all, will be a mere shell of what it was or what it could have been. The financial burdens alone will crush us as we lose everything in the blink of an eye. Most of our dreams, goals, and ambitions will come to ruin. The wounds may be too great and the pain too deep for our family to bear."

Which Way Will You Run?

As we've been learning, a surefire way to weaken your pursuit of God is to strengthen your pursuit of sin. But the reverse is also true: **A surefire way to weaken your pursuit of sin is to strengthen your pursuit of God.**

Regardless of how far you've fallen, repent and renew your relationship with Him — wait on Him no matter how long it takes: *"He acts for the one who waits for Him" (Isa. 64:4)*. Yes, there are consequences for past mistakes, but it's best to live within God's healing arms of forgiveness rather than to live broken outside of His will. Which way will you run?

Chapter Four: Pride

Pride's Explosion is Far-Reaching

"The pride of your heart has deceived you"
(Obadiah 1:3)

Let me state up front that I'm quite aware of my own shortcomings as a pastor. We all struggle with something, but do we humble ourselves and repent, or do we continue to quench and grieve the Spirit because of pride? The difference is life-changing!

One of the major landmines a pastor must avoid at all costs is the deceptive nature of pride. To talk about pride, we must first define it. Basically, pride is a pleasurable emotion characterized by a sense of satisfaction in one's identity, appearance, performance, or accomplishments. Puritan Thomas Tuke made an incredible statement in the 1600s that puts pride into perspective.

> "If a humble man becomes proud of his humility, he loses the very humility he claims to possess and becomes puffed

up with pride. If a man takes pride in his beauty, he forfeits true beauty and becomes a vain fool. If a man is proud of his wisdom, he turns into a fool; if he boasts of his wit, he becomes as senseless as a donkey. If he is proud of his poverty, he becomes rich only in pride; if he is proud of his riches, he becomes poor in piety. What a terrible and hateful sin pride is! Not only is it evil in itself, but it also corrupts good things, turning them into evil. Just as venomous creatures transform whatever they consume into poison, so pride turns all the thoughts, words, and deeds of a proud man into instruments of vanity and self-glorification."[8]

After reading Tuke's comments on pride, what stood out to you? That's probably the very thing that God wants to deal with in your life. Pride manifests in pastoral ministry in many ways such as in preaching or teaching style, education, church size or budget, and so on. As John Stott once declared, "The chief occupational hazard of leadership is pride." Samuel Rutherford adds, "Be not proud of race, face, place, or grace." Deal with pride before it deals with you! **A mistake that makes you humble is better than an achievement that makes you arrogant.**

Pride is not only painful for us but also for those around us. It causes a husband to demean, a father to abuse, and a leader to fall. Pride crushes joy, leads to continual conflicts, and fuels bitterness. My heart is broken by what we are currently witnessing from many pulpits. Without humility, which leads to the fullness of the Spirit, we can easily become weak and carnal or abusive and spiritually dead. *Pride acts as a barrier to genuine repentance because it clouds our vision, and we don't see our need for humility.*

---

[8] Thomas Tuke, *Love to God*, (Crossville, TN: Puritan Publications, 2025) pg. 93.

In every case, we need to embrace the cry of Psalm 85:6, "Will you not revive us again, that your people may rejoice in you?" That must be our plea as well as our passion. One thing is certain: "You can have no greater sign of confirmed pride than when you think you are humble enough" (William Law).

The Day God Broke Me: *Embrace the Pain*

In 2005, I was reading three different books on systematic theology, and many of Spurgeon's works. I could quote Calvin, Luther, and Knox, but God was about ready to knock my block off because of pride.

My mom finally came to me and said, "Son, you have lots of head knowledge, but no one wants to be around you!" I shot back like any good Pharisee would, "They're just convicted!" But deep down in my heart, I knew that she was right: "Knowledge had puffed me up" (cf. 1 Cor. 8:1). Then, through a series of events (including a journal entry from my wife saying the same things), God broke me.

I was very angry because the truth hurts, and pride hates to be lovingly challenged. But I began to realize that she was absolutely correct. I was prideful, controlling, unteachable, and very eager to argue. In my world, I was always right because I was well-read and my studies focused on holiness: "The sin of pride is so ingrained in us that even when other sins decrease, pride grows" (Josiah Shute).

This encounter, along with a few other experiences, truly humbled me. Although pride is still a struggle, I finally understood A.W. Tozer's words: "It is doubtful whether God can bless a man greatly until He has hurt him deeply." Embrace the pain: **Let God break you in order to remake you.**

The Root Cause of Most Problems

Large churches can easily develop pride in what they've accomplished, and smaller churches run the risk of romanticizing their low attendance as a sign of spiritual exclusivity (and, of course, that's why attendance is low). The truth is: God builds a ministry, not us. Since many churches are not located in densely populated metropolitan areas, simple math naturally limits numerical growth. We need to be faithful where God has called us to be.

I know many large church pastors who are humble, and God is using them in powerful ways. I also know many small church pastors whose character and steadfastness should be an example to us all. **The size of the church isn't the problem; the size of the pride in the heart is the problem.** The root cause of most of our problems is pride, and the only way to chip away at pride is with the hammer of humility.

I recently saw an online survey that said 77% of Christians want a church with fewer than 300 members, and 54% want one with fewer than 200 members. The post concluded, "The desire for a 'big church' is not the desire of the people." Regardless of whether you agree or not, the results are telling.[9]

This may be why God allows problems and struggles — do we humble ourselves and become teachable while seasoning our words with grace, or do we love to argue and debate? You can learn a lot about a person when they are challenged or go through adversity: Do they respond with love or react with anger?

---

[9] https://x.com/dalepartridge/status/1907448264578007240?s=46

The enemy of our soul doesn't care what denomination we belong to; he is set on destroying us if pride is left unchecked. We should never be excited about accusing our brothers or arguing over non-essentials. Confrontation must flow from a broken, humble heart that is focused on unity.

If you've been in the ministry for any length of time, you've heard about the landmines of "gold, glory, and girls." Although there is a practical application that can be applied for each of those, the root problem in all three is the landmine of pride. Pride says, "I will never commit adultery." Humility says, "By the grace of God, I haven't, but I can." Knowing you "can" keeps you on guard.

Money and popularity are twin engines of pride, while humility remains the key to God's favor, but sadly, it's the exception rather than the rule. Just look at all the well-known pastors who have fallen in our generation — nine times out of ten, they don't fully repent, but instead, they minimize what they did, and sadly, they try to hop right back into ministry as quickly as possible. That reveals pride and vainglory.

Pride Makes Us Backslide

In an article I wrote years ago titled, _7 Reasons Why Christian Leaders Fall,_ I noted that leaders often fail to shore up blind spots because of pride. Each of us is drawn away by our own evil desires and enticed. When these desires are continually acted upon, they lead to sin (cf. Jas. 1:14-15).

Sin has a life cycle — it either grows or withers depending on whether we feed or starve it. The prolific Puritan author John

Owen wrote, *"Be killing sin, or sin will be killing you."* If you haven't figured it out yet, pride is the root of most problems.[10]

1. Pride tells us that a certain sin will never happen to us. However, First Corinthians 10:12 reminds us that when we think that we are standing firm, that's exactly when we need to be careful. "Pride goes before destruction, a haughty spirit before a fall" (Pro. 16:18). Strength is found in admitting our weaknesses and then shoring up those weaknesses: "For when I am weak, I am strong" (2 Cor. 12:10).

Pride ignores conviction and opens the door to compromise as well as unwise decisions. Conviction is not always a hammer blow to the head, but often a still, small voice to the heart. C.H. Spurgeon rightly noted, "We are never, never so much in danger of being proud as when we think we are humble." Sadly, many confuse God's patience with His approval.

Something that has always amazed me is how pastors can continue preaching and leading even when caught in unrepentant sin. They can still use their gift to preach, sometimes with power, and wrongly assume that everything is ok. When challenged about their heretical beliefs, worldly practices, or hidden sin, they often shoot back: "But look at the fruit!" *Sadly, they're confusing God's patience with His approval, and the success won't continue.*

If this is you, repent and pursue God again via daily brokenness. You might argue, "But that may cost me my ministry." It may, but it will cost a great deal more later. You'd be amazed at what God will do with a humble heart.

---

[10] If reading the ebook, click here to listen to my interview with a pastor who fell and how he got back on track. Or search for the title, *Fall Forward and Fight Again*, on my social media outlets, including my podcast: *Pastor's Unplugged.*

2. Pride says, "I'm too busy." We are all susceptible to putting God second and making ministry our top priority. If we're too busy to cultivate a prayer life that places God first, then we're too busy – period. Men would live better if they prayed better. We're often too busy because we're doing too much. As a result of being too busy, the anchor of prayer is pulled up, and we drift away. "When faith ceases to pray, it ceases to live" (E.M. Bounds).

Moral failure cannot easily gain a stronghold in a broken, praying heart that spends time in the Word and obedience to it (cf. Jas. 1:22). It's hard to fall when you're always on your knees. Nine times out of ten, when a ministry leader falls, they have no meaningful prayer life or devotional practice. In their eyes, they've "arrived."

It has been well stated that "pride is a barrier to all spiritual progress" (Harry Ironside). And Spurgeon rightly noted: "None are more unjust in their judgments of others than those who have a high opinion of themselves."

While on this topic, let's not overlook the minor details, such as not returning texts, emails, or other correspondence, as well as our overall attitude toward people. I truly believe that God will show Himself merciful when we are merciful to others (cf. 2 Sam. 22:26).

Although not always the case, ignoring people can be a form of pride: Being "too busy" is standard protocol for CEOs, but not for pastors.

3. Pride downplays (or misapplies) holiness. Throughout all of biblical history, Satan has always attempted to draw God's people away from His holy standard, and the enemy's tactics have not changed. I vividly remember a story of a young boy who kept falling out of his bed. He finally asked his mother why he kept falling. She wisely answered, "It's because you don't stay far enough in." In the same way, many of us fall back into sin because we don't get far enough into God's framework of safety and protection via holiness. In the words of Isaac Watts, "True Christianity, where it reigns in the heart, will make itself appear in the purity of life."

Of all the attributes of God described in the Bible, holiness is seen most often. Holiness is a vital weapon of defense against the enemy's attack (cf. Eph. 6:14). But holiness must come from brokenness and humility, not legalism.

A low (or wrong) view of holiness always damages morality; we rationalize instead of repent. Holiness born from legalism feeds pride and starves humility. I'm convinced that today's media plays a significant role in the decline of holiness in our churches, as well as in our own lives. Sadly, Hollywood, not the Holy Spirit, influences many. We cannot fill our mind with darkness all week and expect the light of Christ to shine in our lives.

4. Pride *plays* with sexual immorality rather than flees from it. We must be on high alert in this area and have strict accountability measures in place. The devil doesn't show those involved in counseling appointments, inner office meetings, and private "fellowship" the pain and anguish and the years of regret that moral failure brings; he deceives them with a false sense of freedom in ministry, so they simply think they are "helping" the other person.

If you are married but attracted to another person, or if the potential exists, take steps now to remove yourself from that environment. Adultery begins with small compromises. We're often too smart to take deliberate plunges, but, because of pride, we're easily enticed to take one step at a time, one compromise at a time, one bad choice at a time until we're at the bottom. Humility quickly repents and returns to God. Don't entertain sexual immorality: flee from it, and that includes pornography (cf. 1 Cor. 6:18).

5. We fail to strengthen weak areas. The demands of life often tempt us to seek gratification in things that are destructive. We must be on high alert. The enemy uses "opportune times" to draw us away from God. (Luk. 4:13.) The line is so thin that it is often hard to determine when we cross over. Weak areas such as drugs, alcohol, pain meds, sex, anger, marriage issues, and so on are "opportune times" for the enemy to strike. We must expose these areas through repentance, and install safeguards and accountability: To be forewarned is to be forearmed.

6. Accountability is often breached or minimized. Accountability is a safeguard, but it's not bulletproof. Accountability, by itself, doesn't work — it's not realistic to ask others to hold you accountable. Your heart must be focused on honoring God's Word. Accountability simply adds another level of security in the battle against sin. It's healthy to say to those we trust, "I'm struggling in this area. Can you pray with me and ask the hard questions from time to time?" This is the primary reason I believe that a plurality of godly elders is the best way to lead a church, with the lead pastor being the "leader among equals."

Yes, I've heard of horror stories of renegade elders, but the greatest number of fallen pastors often come from a church hierarchy where they are at the top, with a board beneath them. This is also a HUGE pitfall for ministries led by one man who has no one to keep him accountable. Yes, there is a "board," but most of the board members don't live nearby and are not involved in the ministry's day-to-day operations. As I'm writing this, I just heard a leaked audio from a megachurch pastor harshly berating his staff. I couldn't believe my ears — he sounded more like a CEO than a shepherd. A plurality of elders would have helped keep him accountable and deflated his ego.

Additionally, consider adding accountability software that sends a weekly report of all questionable websites you visited to your wife's email. Also, leave your phone out each day for transparency. This is a major deterrent, and it makes you very conscious of even seemingly innocent sites or texts. *To the pride-filled heart, this may seem extreme, but humility says otherwise.* We need to be armed against the enemy who steals, kills, and destroys. The greater our influence, the greater the need for accountability: spiritually, financially, and relationally.

The enemy loves to work in darkness and deceit. Exposing cracks in the armor helps others keep an eye on them as well.

7. Pride excuses wrong behavior and fosters a sense of entitlement. Ministry is hard and can easily take its toll. Feeling a sense of entitlement (fueled by pride) is often the beginning of justifying wrong choices. We can become jealous and judgmental of those who seem to "have it all." But always remember Oswald Chambers's words: "God buries His men in the midst of paltry things; no monuments are erected to them; they are ignored, not because they are unworthy, but because they are in the place where they cannot be seen."

Luke 16:10 should be a great encouragement as it promotes a humble heart: "So you also, when you have done everything you were told to do, should say, 'We are unworthy servants; we have only done our duty'." Sin can be silenced in a thankful, broken heart that is set on worshiping God. God has given us the privilege to serve Him, proclaim His truth, and help others. Don't allow frustration and negativity to fuel pride and lead you down the wrong path.

Pride Also Fuels the Spirit of Accusation

Due to the internet's ability to spread a HUGE amount of information quickly, it's easier than ever to expose sin publicly. Exposure is sorely needed and long overdue, but on the other hand, it can become very destructive when arrogant and judgmental people use it as a weapon. To truly change lives, truth must be seasoned with grace and watered with hope.

Instead of pointing people to hope and restoration, we often rush to premature judgment: "Guilty Until Proven Innocent!" Many outlets that profit from "clickbait" are eager to drag someone through the mud again and again and again. Because of pride, many of us can become cold, callous, and overly critical in our zeal for justice. We may be right in our reasoning, yet wrong in our hearts.

I'm assuming that the reader understands that I'm not lumping everything into the same category. A leader who abuses children should be handled much differently than a leader who steps down due to anger and a controlling attitude. When victims are involved, we must listen carefully and prioritize their issues. Pride focuses on self-preservation, while humility focuses on self-denial.

We must provide a safe, non-threatening environment for victims to come forward, but also avoid the *spirit of accusation* behind some of these so-called "ministries" who love pulling others down. Because of pride, I've personally seen false accusations hurt good, godly people. Once more, I'm not minimizing abuse — it must be dealt with swiftly — but we must be careful that arrogance and *the spirit of accusation* don't kill our discernment.

One particular ministry comes to mind: Years ago, a pastor had to step down due to his aggressive leadership style, but some Christian outlets still criticize him to this day without considering the possibility that he may have been humbled and broken by God. **"True repentance is when a man grieves for his sin to the extent that he abandons it" (Josiah Shute).** We should champion this rather than disdain it.

Where's the compassion? Where's erring on the side of grace? Unless we have evidence proving otherwise, why aren't we rejoicing that God has done a great work in the man's heart?

Humility Hears Both Sides

Has *the spirit of accusation* and the lack of humility and brokenness crept into your own heart? I've been guilty of this myself. When we recognize this, we must repent. Proverbs 18:17 reminds us that the first person to "plead his cause seems right, until his neighbor comes and examines him." We also must acknowledge Proverbs 28:11, which says we should not form opinions without hearing both sides. Pride often prevents us from pursuing the truth.

To adequately assess situations, the critic contending for the truth must be *filled* with the Spirit to display the *fruit* of the Spirit. Sadly, that's not the case with many of these so-called "discernment ministries" that are fueled by pride and motivated by revenue. It's very hard to speak with clarity and precision when we only have snapshots of a story.

Sadly, many of these outlets do a lot of dirty work behind the scenes, baiting people for evidence that might not even be valid — looking for exposure rather than truth. Take heed: Not only will fallen leaders be held accountable, but so will heresy hunters who are operating from a wrong spirit.

Leaders need to be more forthright and admit their sin. People would respect them a lot more, and it would set a good example. **Leaders not only lead by example with integrity but also with repentance.**

To briefly recap: Pride deceives, hardens, destroys, and hurts, but humility enlightens, softens, builds, and heals. The choice is yours. We are watchmen, not rock stars. *We must be part of the solution rather than the problem, and it all begins with humility.*

Are You *Contentiously* Contending?

Sadly, another area of pride for pastors is head knowledge. **Many are often *continuously* contending for the truth instead of continually humbling themselves before God.** But, on the other end of the spectrum are liberal pastors who are doing a great deal of damage because they are failing to lead people to God. They often make decisions based on not offending others, never stopping to consider that they are offending God by their silence about sin.

As a result of this tension between conservative and less conservative churches, the church today finds itself in an interesting spot. We are commanded to love all people who struggle with sin, yet we cannot affirm sin nor turn a blind eye to the unrepentant practices of those who claim to be Christ's followers. Sadly, liberals are considered "mainstream," while those who support the tenets of Scripture are called "mean-spirited." Up is down, and down is up. Right is wrong, and wrong is right.

Pastors, if you are *digressing* from the truth, please don't call it *progress*. Liberals need to repent of apathy and a low view of Scripture, and conservatives need to repent if pride is a stronghold in their lives.

Here are a few questions to consider:

1. Do you always have to be right, prove your point, or get the last word in?
2. Are you often defensive and moody?
3. Are you quick to talk and slow to listen?
4. Are your words seasoned with rebuke more than grace?
5. Are you unteachable and eager to dispute?
6. Do you often make "non-essentials" essential?
7. Are you too busy (too important) to return texts and emails?
8. Do you take issue with some of God's Word? Are you doubting some of it or taking issue with what you refer to as "outdated morality"?
9. Did you want to gloss over or avoid this chapter?

If you answered yes to any of the above questions (like I have in the past), then pride may be a problem.

Grow in the Soil of Humility

Pride blinds us spiritually, as illustrated in the life of a famous celebrity. As the story goes, a flight attendant asked this celebrity to buckle his seat belt before the plane took off. He shot back, "Superman don't need no seat belt!" To that, she replied, "Superman don't need no airplane!"

Obadiah 1:3 reminds us that pride can deceive us. And, with some exceptions, the younger you are, the more careful you need to be. First Timothy 3:6 says that a leader should not be a novice. This doesn't necessarily have to do with age, but it often does. Normally, the older we are, the more we've been through in regard to brokenness and pain, and hopefully, our ministry is growing in the soil of humility. If you're a young pastor, please plant your heart into the soil of humility now before it's too late.

If you were like me when I planted the church, you may have also had unrealistic goals, such as growing a large church in a short amount of time. Church planters often think, "I'm going to do things the right way," and they often pull down the church they are leaving. **When the landmine of pride explodes, the damage is far-reaching.**

When God Builds a Church

There is nothing wrong when God grows a ministry, even quickly, but we have to be careful that pride has not crept in. (Note the words: "when God grows"; that's the *key*). When I broke out of my season of discouragement, I thanked God over and over again for the pace at which He grew the ministry. Looking back, if the church had grown very quickly, I don't think my character would have provided a strong enough foundation.

Sadly, that's what we often see today: A charismatic pastor plants a church in a highly populated area, but sadly, the church grows faster than his character. Because of the incredible growth, he thinks that he is truly God's man, and pride begins to tighten its deadly grip. He fails to realize that the growth might just be a numbers game: A church + a good communicator + a highly populated area = growth.

In many cases, but not always, this type of pastor is inclined to be soft on doctrine, avoid confrontation, and side-step difficult topics. Why? Because he built the ministry, not God, and what it takes to build a ministry is what it takes to keep it going. But, when God builds a church at the right pace, using a pastor filled with the Spirit who boldly preaches the unchanging truth of His Word, the church is spiritually healthy.

In closing, recognize and avoid the landmine of pride at all costs. **G.K. Chesterton once said, "If I had only one sermon to preach, it would be a sermon against pride."**

Make sure that you plant your church in the soil of humility and continue to water it with brokenness: *"God can do more in a moment than you can ever do in a lifetime" (Ronnie Floyd)*. It's been well stated over the years that pride must die in you before heaven can live in you. To truly succeed in ministry, humility has to be your goal.

Chapter Five: Pain

God Breaks You to Remake You

"We are hard-pressed on every side, yet not crushed;
we are perplexed, but not in despair"
(2 Corinthians 4:8)

Early in my ministry, I read the following in Charles Spurgeon's famous book, *Lectures to My Students*: "If you can do anything else, do it. If you can stay out of the ministry, stay out of the ministry."

At the time, I remember thinking, "Wow, the 1800s when Spurgeon lived must have been a difficult time. I'm sure that doesn't apply now." Boy, was I wrong! Of all the things I underestimated going into the ministry, it was the amount of pain it would produce. Whether it's relational pain, criticism, burnout, disappointment in ministry, health issues, or personal struggles, it takes its toll.

At times, the pain can be unbearable. When left unchecked, pain turns into discouragement, and we can easily become bitter. Bitter men become angry and isolated men, which can lead to a difficult work environment for staff and an unloving experience for members. Wives become emotional punching bags, and kids begin to doubt God when their father doesn't exhibit the same joy that he preaches about.

Noted author and speaker Josh McDowell once said, "One of the most common questions I get is, 'How can we live for Christ, when we don't want the Christ that our parents have'?" What a powerful reminder to not let pain poison our hearts, especially because leaders who hold in pain are more likely to fall into sexual immorality or addiction to numb the pain.

The Beauty and Blessing of Brokenness

As stated in the Introduction: Pastoring is a hard calling because our lives, and the lives of our wives and children, are constantly on display for the world to see. We've been hurt so much that the walls we build to protect us can eventually imprison us. **But in the midst of pain, God often does something beautiful.**

Although it hurts, brokenness, like setting a bone, can eventually strengthen us. Moses spent years on the backside of the desert as God broke and prepared him. Isaiah was completely broken when he cried, "Woe to me! I am ruined! .... my eyes have seen the King, the LORD Almighty" (Isa. 6:5). Jeremiah collapsed and cried out, "My soul will weep in secret" (13:17).

The Psalms are saturated with the brokenness of David, and Paul had to be knocked to the ground and have his eyes blinded by the glory of God before true humility became a hallmark of his ministry. Throughout the Bible, brokenness was the hammer that God used and is still using today. *Broken pride results in beautiful humility.*

I'll never forget the day that I read the following quote by A.W. Tozer: **"It is doubtful whether God can bless a man greatly until He has hurt him deeply."** I was going through a very difficult season, and I soon realized that God was breaking me down to build me back up. I was at a turning point: I could become bitter and resentful or humble myself and grow from the experience. This is where the majority of pastors find themselves today: Instead of getting better, we become bitter. *Instead of emptying ourselves to be filled with the Spirit, we tend to be full of pride and selfish ambition. This needs to change.*

We must continually take our thoughts captive and remind ourselves that pain is part of God's calling. Like the limp that wouldn't leave Jacob or the thorn that kept Paul humble, the beauty and blessing of brokenness is that it can act like a magnet, drawing you closer to God. But if you are the main cause of your pain, then repent immediately and apologize, even if you think the other person should carry some of the responsibility. We must be the better person and pursue reconciliation whenever possible (cf. Rom. 12:18). We don't have to take all the responsibility, unless warranted, but we often need to initiate reconciliation. Saying, "I could have handled that better. Would you forgive me?" goes a long way. **Often, your humility will crack the armor of defense that the other person is wearing.**

God is no respecter of persons, but He is a respecter of principles, and the principle of brokenness is profound.

Pressure Helps Us Go Low

When you become bitter, you lose intimacy with God, boldness, purpose, and the Spirit's fire. Return to Him, and He will return to you (Zec. 1:3). **The strength of your church is in its purity and spiritual power fueled by brokenness, not in its numbers.** God allows us to experience the pressure of pain so we go down on our knees. Pain can reshape your prayer life. Prayer can no longer be a footnote at the end of a sermon; instead, prayer and worship must guide the church through these critical times, and pain can help us get there.

Focusing on humility is a must. How can God fill a heart already crowded with self — self-willed, self-sufficient, self-made? Self must die and brokenness is the undertaker. We need to be a champion for unity and swallow pride; the rewards will be amazing. Conversely, when we dig our heels in and become angry and defensive, the outcome is never good.

Granted, there are times when we need to be firm, but to be truly effective, firmness must flow from brokenness. We need boldness and brokenness; we need the hammer of God and the humility of the Spirit. We need more thunder in the pulpits, but we also need more brokenness in our hearts.

When we provide the sacrifice of humility, God often provides the fire of the Spirit and our ministry flourishes. We must weep before we whip (Leonard Ravenhill). Don't be misled by "likes," "followers," and "shares." **Popularity doesn't always equate to spiritual success.** We must watch out for *affirmation-based identity, and* instead, find our identity in Christ and His calling on our lives.

Pain Can Strengthen Faith

How does pain increase faith? When we persevere regardless of our feelings and trust God despite the pain, our faith flourishes. In essence, we are saying, "Lord, I don't understand this, but I trust You. Will You help me through it?" **His sovereignty must be your sanity.** Again, God often uses pain to build faith and shape character. We become much better pastors when we grow from the pain. John Durant once wrote, "Blessed are we when God's corrections are our lessons, His punishments our teachers, His chastisements our guidance."

If pain doesn't lead us to our Savior, it will lead us to sin. Faith produces obedience by overcoming. Questioning what God is doing is part of the journey. Faith doesn't always "feel" it or "see" it so we walk in faith. As Steve Schell once noted, "If you knew, with absolute certainty, that something would work out, it wouldn't be faith." Oswald Chambers adds, "God doesn't give us overcoming life, He gives us life as we overcome ... If we take the initiative to overcome, we will find that we have the inspiration of God, because He immediately gives us the power of life."

Wow! So much truth in those two quotes. Just as an athlete embraces pain to succeed or a muscle to grow, we too must allow pain to build our spiritual muscle. The choice is yours.

Set Your Face Like a Flint

One verse that really helps me through difficult seasons is Isaiah 50:7: "For the Lord God will help Me; therefore I will not be disgraced; therefore I have set My face like a flint, and I know that I will not be ashamed." As most know, this foretold of Jesus setting His face like a solid rock (flint) toward Calvary. But we too must set our face like a flint through the difficult challenges. "I'm going forward regardless" must be our motto.

During my journey, I often read Second Chronicles 15:7: "But you be strong and do not become weak, and your work will be rewarded." I also read Second Samuel 30:6, where David strengthened himself in the Lord. David lived it before he could write it. *God has called us to be shepherds to the shattered, rebuilders of the broken, a place of worship for the wounded.* **We cannot take people through their journey of pain if we ourselves have not traveled on the same dusty road.**

The Word must transform your heart, or pain will darken it. And when we worship, pray, and meditate on God's promises, pain is turned into praise, bitterness into thankfulness, and disappointment into joy. Seeking God is the only way to offset the toxic damage that pain can bring to our body, soul, and spirit.

Does pain push you down on your knees in prayer and praise, or does it derail you? What do you do when your dreams die? Do you become bitter, or do you praise Him? What about when friends bail, people lie, and heresy-hunters slander your ministry? Do you learn and grow or consistently defend and argue?

Have we drifted so far that we have forgotten to exhibit the same grace that we so desperately need ourselves? Hurt people hurt people, and many of us will end up hurting the very people we are called to help. The key is to put on the garment of praise *now* before the spirit of heaviness wears you down: "Justifiable resentment can eat you alive" (Stephen Arterburn).

A Misunderstood Calling

Leaders walk a very fine line: We must be bold but also broken, firm but flexible, hard on sin but humble with others, demanding excellence but not pushy, motivating but not overbearing. Unfortunately, it's impossible to walk this line perfectly. We need to own our faults, apologize, and ask God to change us. But on the flip side, a wounded pastor who is constantly under the microscope — where every word and action is weighed in the balances — can become passive in order to avoid pain. We begin to think, "I don't want to deal with that issue; I've been hurt many times before," and we become paralyzed.

The passive pastor gets steamrolled, and the abusive pastor is the steamroller. Pastors will spend their lives trying to find the middle ground. Those who are abusive, manipulating, and controlling (the wrong type of control, that is) need to repent and seek restoration, and rebuild broken relationships. Passive, weak, people-pleasing pastors also need to repent and spend time in the prayer closet. Ask God for boldness to lead, fortitude to make tough decisions, and the strength to continue. Bold, humble, gracious leaders are needed in these dire times. The church, as well as our nation, desperately needs to hear "the voice crying in the wilderness" to awaken, convict, and restore. It's hard to walk the fine line between passivity and passion, balance and boldness. As they say, "The struggle is real."

Because pastoring is very unique — you're the leader, often referred to as the "boss" — it can be very challenging to pastor our friends and build strong relationships with those in our congregation. This tension often leads to a great deal of pain. Other leaders may want your position, trusted friends don't want you to speak the truth into their lives, and staff often feel awkward around the leader. It's important to navigate these challenges with grace, humility, and understanding.

As a child, I would isolate myself to prevent future pain (I still tend to do that on some level even now). I became an approval seeker, something you might find hard to believe if you heard my preaching. Angry people scared me, and personal criticism hurt more deeply than it should. The deep pains of ministry can linger, and the enemy of our soul will use them against us. For this reason, I try not to post things on social media when I'm in pain. I've made this mistake many times over the years.

Now, a word of encouragement: Leaders may appear controlling because they are called to lead. They may come across as harsh because they set boundaries. They may be viewed as hard because they are called to defend. They may appear secretive because they must choose their words carefully. As leaders, if we are not available 24/7, people say that we are "not there for them." If we can't make every event or respond to every email, Tweet, and Facebook post, we are labeled as "unapproachable." This is to be expected and shouldn't cause much pain as long as we remember this.

Thankfully, God makes provision for all our needs through His Word. He must be our anchor and our true source of hope. Understanding your calling is a great help when it comes to managing pain.

Don't Let Discouragement Discourage Worship

I was scrolling through X one day and saw a post that sums up much of what I want to say. I don't know the writer, but their words nailed it: "For those who have been contending long and hard for a particular breakthrough, there is a spiritual asset often overlooked that is just as important as your prayers, praises, and proclamations: Perseverance."

They continued, "To persevere means to keep walking when others have stopped. To keep going and looking for the light even when you're still in the dark. It's the ability to not quit; a determination to defy the odds and outlast the doubts." They finished with, **"Perseverance may be the one asset that reveals the true measure of your faith in God."**[11] Wow, a thousand times over!

The Christian life is always under siege. Pain is like an emotional seesaw, adding just enough weight to keep us balanced with humility. The next time pain pushes down and adds weight to your life, and you feel weak and heavy-laden, simply give it to the Lord. Taking our thoughts captive is actually where success is found. What our mind thinks, our heart feels. Picture in your mind that God is allowing this emotional weight to balance praise and pain.

When pastors become too puffed up with pride, God often uses pain to deflate their egos. Like a physical seesaw without a balanced weight, the other side will come crashing down and may cause injury. Pain will often test our spiritual strength–we must get used to it. In darkness, will we still praise Him? In depression, will we still seek Him? In discouragement, will we still follow Him? **In disappointment, will we still worship, in sorrow still surrender, and in sadness still serve Him?**

A text from a friend of mine, who had led worship at an event I spoke at years ago, reminded me just how much God honors commitment and perseverance, regardless of how we feel. We were both expecting a large event, but there were only a few dozen people there. We hadn't talked about this event since it

---

[11] Although I can't find the post on X anymore, I believe it was posted by Wanda Alger.

occurred, but I just happened to tell him how I pressed through that night, and God really blessed the message. He texted back:

> "The sound system was horrible, and there was no one there. They all looked at me like 'What is this?' I was embarrassed. But I said, 'Let's just get up there and give God our best.' In my heart I felt like this sucks. But the strangest thing happened: As soon as I stepped to the mic, I felt God's presence so strong. Then, as we were singing, I was in awe. There were only 25 people. But it sounded like there were 500 people singing! The Holy Spirit's presence was so heavy in that place. It was crazy. When we finished, the band was in shock. They heard what I heard and felt what I felt. We were all humbled and grateful to be in His presence."

Again, never let discouragement stop you from worshiping. The more you seek Him, the more you'll find Him.

The Shepherd of the Shattered

In closing, we need to remember that *broken crayons still color.* God is the Shepherd of the shattered and the rebuilder of the broken. God breaks us to rebuild us so we can help others, but we must humble ourselves so the Potter can shape the clay, or an eleven-day journey through the wilderness may take us forty years (cf. Jos. 5:6).

We must let our pain crucify our pride. He rebuilds the broken, elevates the humble, and restores the wounded. We can rebuild the breach and strengthen what remains, but we must pray this today: **"O God, take me, break me, and remake me."**

Poor Health Hinders Productivity

"But I discipline my body and bring it into subjection, lest, when I have preached to others, I myself should become disqualified" (1 Corinthians 9:27)

"Why would I include a chapter on this topic?" you may ask. Because it's vitally important: 1) A lack of discipline in this area leads to a lack of discipline in other areas, 2) health plays an enormous and significant role in productivity, energy, and attitude, and it deeply affects our emotional health. *Trust me, you feel so much better when you're controlling your desires rather than allowing your desires to control you.* 3) Fitness is not being discussed very often in the church, and it needs to be. Congregations, their children, and their pastors are sicker than previous generations, and very few are helping them heal.

The physical affects the spiritual. Don't believe me? Try getting just a few hours of sleep for a few nights, eat lots of junk food loaded with caffeine and sugar, pop a Xanax before preaching, and see how you feel.

No! Don't do this — you get my point: **If you don't make time for health, you should probably make time for illness.**

Something We Don't Talk About

It's been well-stated that food is the most abused drug, while fasting remains the most forgotten cure, and exercise is the most underrated antidepressant. The stark reality is that the number one cause of most illnesses stems from a pervasive apathy — people either don't care about their health or, even when they do, they fail to take meaningful action, a trend that sadly includes many pastors.

You are closest to operating at full capacity when you focus on both physical and spiritual health. **If you think that health is too hard and expensive, wait until you get the bill for regret!**

As we all know, our main priority needs to be spiritual health; our relationship with God is the only foundation on which we must build our lives. However, on top of that foundation lies some very important building materials such as a healthy marriage, wise financial stewardship, fatherhood, and so on. To fulfill our purpose and be productive, we also need to focus on our physical health.

Albert N. Martin wrote in his helpful book for pastors, *The Man of God,* that we should focus on physical and emotional health. He adds that we must "engage in a regular but flexible discipline aimed at keeping your redeemed humanity in optimum health and vigor."[12] We should not allow a lack of self-discipline to

---

[12] Pg. 303

continually feed carnal appetites. Recall the verses that I shared in an earlier chapter: In First Corinthians 9:27, Paul disciplined his body to avoid being disqualified from preaching, and Proverbs 5:23 warns that an undisciplined life can lead to death, and that a man without self-control is like a city broken into and left without walls (Pro. 25:28).

Not "If' but "When"

We should glorify God in our whole body, not just in certain parts. Many, from John Owen to John Wesley and countless other preachers, regretted not focusing more on their health. Preaching is a combination of everything we are and do, both positively and negatively. God gave us an incredible temple that we are to honor Him with (cf. 1 Cor. 6:19-20). A healthy lifestyle assists our calling.

You may be young, enjoying your double espresso latte with a donut before you head to lunch later at a fast food restaurant, but trust me, it *will* catch up to you. **It's not *if* a poor diet will hinder us, *but when* it will.** It's also affecting you right now more than you realize. What we do with our health *today* sets the stage for *what we'll experience a decade later.* In other words, how you treat your health at age forty will have huge ramifications at age fifty, and so on.

For this reason, this chapter focuses primarily on physical health, as physical disciplines can also affect spiritual health. If just a 5-day junk food binge can negatively affect the brain and contribute to the development of obesity and many other related health issues, can you imagine a *lifestyle* focused on it?[13]

---

[13] Scientists Say Eating Junk Food For Just A Few Days Can Alter Your Brain: https://www.nature.com/articles/s42255-025-01226-9

Out of Context

To begin our journey, we need to stop using First Timothy 4:8 out of context. In saying that "bodily exercise profits a little, but godliness is profitable for all things," Paul was not suggesting that our health doesn't matter; he was emphasizing the importance of spiritual growth over mere physical fitness.

Stewarding our health is foundational, but few books written for pastors address it. Just because many authors and pastors don't talk about this topic doesn't mean we shouldn't discuss it, especially when our physical health plays a significant role in our spiritual productivity.

In other words, the choices we make, such as not getting enough sleep, staying addicted to caffeine, sugar, alcohol, etc., as well as consuming harmful foods and chemicals, definitely affect our spiritual health — more so than you may realize. **A lack of self-discipline always hurts us spiritually.** *This topic is so important that I would encourage some pastors to take a mini-sabbatical to pray, fast, and reset their health.*

Competing Against King Stomach

There are three primary reasons why we don't discuss stewarding our health and dethroning King Stomach:[14]

1. Spiritual health is more important than physical health, so we simply don't talk about it. But again, this is flawed reasoning: Everything we do in life is either enhanced or harmed based on our health. Granted, I know that there are those who, through no fault of their own, cannot do anything

---

[14] Jentezen Franklin has coined the phrase King Stomach many times in his fasting books and sermons.

about their health. I'm talking to those who can make changes, and that's the vast majority of us.

2. Most pastors struggle with gluttony and use food as medication. Everyone understands the term "comfort food." It's food that provides a sense of relief and comfort when we are struggling emotionally in stressful situations. Sometimes the relief we experience after eating our favorite comfort foods is due to the effect the food has on our nervous system, and sometimes it's due to certain emotional connections and memories we have with a specific food. It's hard to talk about what we struggle with, especially if we don't want to change. We've become comfortable and faithful subjects under the reign of King Stomach.

3. Most pastors are not educated in health and fitness. As a result, they don't realize how important it is, but that shouldn't stop them from encouraging a healthy lifestyle. The physical health of your congregation is incredibly important. It should be a topic of discussion along with other areas of stewardship. Think about how many times we pray for people, yet fail to realize that a change in their lifestyle could lead to healing for many of them.

What Did an Online Poll Reveal?

While writing this chapter, I did an online poll asking how many people think that churches should avoid serving coffee and donuts. Because of the major health problems that affect most of our members, an astonishing 88% said that we should not aid in the deterioration of their health. *We are called to help, not hurt.* Here are a few points to consider:

- We teach parenting principles, but what if we are too overweight, tired, and sick to spend time with our kids or grandkids?
- We teach healthy marriage principles, but what if spouses are always moody and depressed because of poor health? Wouldn't that take a toll on the marriage?
- We teach about stewarding our finances, but shouldn't we also encourage good health so we can enjoy financial freedom instead of spending the last decade of our lives in an assisted living home?

Failing to take care of our health doesn't sound like good stewardship to me.

Fueling What We Should Be Fighting

I won't shock and alarm you with the number of obese children in America, but we are experiencing a national health crisis, and our silence as leaders speaks volumes. Most of what we and our congregations are struggling with in regard to anxiety, depression, health issues, and so on, are often caused by poor food choices that lead to nutrient deficiencies and toxic overload. Did you catch that? Experts are finding that nutrient deficiency can cause anxiety. **It's definitely not the only cause, but it's a major cause.**

By all means, pray for them, but if some illnesses are caused by gluttony and poor stewardship, then reversing course can get them back on track (cf. Deut. 28:61). Why not have a men's or women's *walk* on Saturdays instead of always sitting at tables drinking too much "Christian Crack" and consuming donuts? Why not offer teachings or studies on biblically based health from time to time?

Health needs to be a priority because many leaders are igniting the disease epidemic instead of helping congregants through it — fueling what we should be fighting.

Granted, I'm well aware of the challenges, and our church does not do things perfectly (nor do I), but shouldn't there be an effort to help people live better? Again, moderation may be fine for some, but most people need to make significant changes to see lasting results.

The System is Clogged and Contaminated

Don't worry, I won't bog you down with technical subjects like mTOR, thermoneutrality, NNMT expression, brain-derived neurotrophic factor, autophagy, and so on — I'll get right to the point with the key things you need to know.

No doubt you've heard the term "insulin resistance" and are aware of the damage that it causes, primarily in regard to type 2 diabetes and many other diseases. Most diseases occur because of what's going on inside our cells. And because of overconsumption, many diseases are linked to the same problem.

When we eat carbohydrates, the body signals the pancreas to release insulin. This is normal, healthy, and good, according to God's design. The insulin seeks out cells and binds to insulin receptors on the cell's surface. This allows glucose to enter the cell through the membrane, providing energy to the cell. So far, so good, right? Not so quick!

Continual overconsumption without periodic seasons of fasting allows excess material to accumulate in the cells, leading to cellular damage. The cells then resist the signal, close the door, and become resistant to insulin. As a result, the glucose stays in the bloodstream, causing significant damage.

Unfortunately, it doesn't stop there. The body tries to force insulin into the cells by producing more, which works in the short term, but eventually takes its toll. Excessive insulin affects the immune system and other parts of the body. Alzheimer's is now being called type 3 diabetes for this very reason. Sadly, many diseases are completely reversible and preventable if we would just take the initiative.[15]

Nobody Cares More than You

First, we must stop the cycle of treating the symptom rather than the cause. Please don't misunderstand — I'm not suggesting that we don't need medication from time to time, but we must understand that in a very high number of cases, medication doesn't cure anything; it simply manages disease and often makes us worse off.

It's been estimated that nearly 75 percent of US clinical trials in medicine are paid for by private companies that benefit. Did you catch that? Why do we use wisdom and discernment when it comes to all other areas of society, but when it comes to our health, we blindly follow? For example, "Take this drug to feel better" — never mind the fact that side effects include internal bleeding, seizures, suicidal thoughts, and panic attacks. We must be diligent and use wisdom. We need

---

[15] Authors and podcasters such as Casey & Calley Means, Dr. Peter Attia, Dr. Ben Bikman, Dr. Valter Longo, Ben Greenfield, Thomas DeLauer, Dr. Paul Saladino, Dr. Gabriella Lyons and others go into much more detail in their resources. But keep in mind that many of them ascribe to evolution, which makes no sense. When you look at health through a biblical lens it makes much more sense.

physicians, and thank God for them, but we also need to educate ourselves and take responsibility for our own health.

As one of many examples, a local doctor wanted to send me home with two different medications for high blood pressure. Before leaving, I asked if he had used the large cuff when he took my pressure. He hadn't. When he did, the blood pressure reading was normal. **Nobody is going to care more about your health than you.**

If you're ready to take back your health, be encouraged that it's not as difficult as it appears. *The key is to focus on direction rather than perfection and to get back up when you fall.* To help you get started, I've listed five tips below. These five areas made an incredible difference in my life, including getting my weight down to a healthy level. As always, consult your physician before starting any program, including fasting.

My Top Five Health Tips

Many researchers are discovering the enormous connection between cellular health and longevity, particularly with healthy mitochondria — the powerhouse of the cell. Here are the top five ways to restore health:

1. FOCUS ON DEEP SLEEP: Deep sleep is when healing and restoration really take place. How can we expect to be healthy if we miss this important area? Sadly, very few people experience deep sleep because they are addicted to alcohol, sugar, caffeine, and food, which deeply affects REM. Some argue, "But I fall right to sleep; these things don't affect me." But that's not deep, healing sleep; it's adrenal fatigue and exhaustion.

We then repeat the process of self-medicating the following day to balance out sleep deprivation. It's a never-ending cycle that we must break if we are to experience true rest. For me, backing off from caffeine played a huge role in better health. Just try stopping and you'll see how hard it is. Sadly, I always excused my poor attitude with statements such as, "I had a bad day ... I'm under a lot of stress ... I'm tired." Ironically, I was the primary cause of my "bad" days, stress, and fatigue because I was consuming too much caffeine, which makes us very irritable and anxious. More in the next point.

2. SEVERELY CURTAIL CAFFEINE: The majority of positive feedback that I've received over the years often centers around this topic — people can't believe how much better they feel when they focus on health and minimize stimulants. Because caffeine runs along the same biochemical pathways in the brain as cocaine, opium, and amphetamines, quitting can be a nightmare. I know that many won't want to hear this, but I have a responsibility to speak the truth in love. If it doesn't apply to you, then great, but I know that it will apply to the lives of many people. Teenagers and young adults also desperately need to know this information. So many of them are spun out on caffeine all day, and it really affects their health, mentally and physically.

My suggestion is to back off gradually, day by day, until your intake is very minimal, and use organic green tea (with light caffeine and L-theanine) whenever possible. You'll be shocked by the results. Granted, the first week may be torture, but it will be worth it.

Psychologists now recognize caffeine-related disorders such as "Caffeine Intoxication," "Caffeine-induced Anxiety Disorder," and "Caffeine-induced Sleep Disorder." These can begin with even minimal doses. Increasing the amount to 500 mg of caffeine (the amount found in approximately 24 ounces of coffee) dramatically increases these symptoms. All this can lead to angry outbursts, panic attacks, severe depression, and extreme irritability.

This begs the question, "How many pastors are suffering mentally and physically simply because of poor health — continuing the addiction rather than removing the cause of the problem?" Not in all cases, but in most cases, depression, anxiety, irritability, and so on, could be severely curtailed if health (spiritual and physical) was a priority.

Cutting back on caffeine was a tremendous help to me because I would fall asleep sooner and more quickly, which allowed me to get up very early and spend that precious time with the Lord. Late-night eating and social media stimuli also prevent deep sleep. I recommend not eating three hours before bed and avoiding electronics for at least one hour. Fix this issue and you'll be well on your way to feeling better. Productivity and energy will both increase substantially.

Granted, if you're truly a night owl and late hours work for you, stick with it. But most people would do much better by going to bed earlier and using the freshness of the morning to prepare their heart before they prepare their schedule. Make sure you're *truly* wired for the later hours, rather than allowing your lifestyle to set the course. The vast majority of late-nighters aren't truly night owls; they've created this schedule by going to bed late, sleeping in, and using caffeine later in the day.

It's not my intent to point solely to stimulants, soft drinks, and energy drinks because there are many other addictive substances; nor is being legalistic my goal: **My heart is to simply share how the most addictive substance in America affects health, and then let you be the judge.**

3. CONSUME LIFE-GIVING FOOD AS OFTEN AS POSSIBLE: Dead processed food from a factory does little to sustain life. We were designed to eat living food that contains the building blocks of life. Vitamins, minerals, phytochemicals, and other nutrients are deposited into the body to renew, restore, and replenish.

The best diet is actually very simple: Choose God-given food in *moderation*, rather than man-made, processed, refined food. But if you're like me, instead of applying some hard work and discipline, you'd rather take a pill, powder, or supplement. I've tried a lot of supplements — everything from creatine and amino acids to NAD and NAC, and from Alpha-Lipoic Acid to natural testosterone boosters. *Although they all have their benefits, nothing (and I mean nothing) works as well as caloric moderation combined with seasons of fasting, along with consuming life-giving food, getting sufficient sleep, and minimizing stress and limiting snacking.*

We can't take more medication or supplements and hope our cells repair themselves. It doesn't work that way: Both food and fasting play huge roles in cellular repair. Additionally, researchers are finding that the new craze of fat loss medications, known as Semaglutides (think Ozempic), can cost the body a significant amount of muscle mass. A very high percentage of people stop the drug and gain weight back. Since they probably won't regain muscle and bone density, they're fatter than when they first began.[16] These drugs have other adverse reactions as well, such as paralyzing the digestive system, not to mention that many people are dependent on them for the rest of their lives. The best way is always God's way.

---

[16] Dr. Ben Bikman breaks it down here. Or search this online: Fat Cell Scientist Reveals Shocking Ozempic Effects that Doctors Don't Explain by Dr. Ben Bikman

If you decide to step out into the diet medication minefield (or other medication), pray and ask God for direction, and also educate yourself. I can't stress this enough. You don't need a medical degree, but you should research both sides of the equation. For example, you may feel at ease about HRT (Hormone Replacement Therapy) or peptide therapy; thankfully, advancements in the medical field have made a difference. But I've also found that the easiest route isn't always the best route, and taking medication has side effects. Most men can naturally increase their testosterone by losing weight, exercising, and eating a balanced diet.

4. FEAST ON FASTING: **Fasting doesn't kill us; overconsumption does.** Disease is often a problem of toxicity created by what we consume, ingest, or breathe — and fasting can be the detox solution. I actually went on an extended fast while writing this book. It took a few days, but I eventually felt good. However, there were also many hard days where I consumed a little food. The power of the made-up mind was the key. I knew I had to do something. (For more, see the footnote where I featured a podcast link on this topic in March 2025).[17]

For tips on how to fast and overcome hunger, along with recommendations on who shouldn't fast and what types of fast to consider, download my two books on fasting for free at WCFAV.org. They go into great detail and answer many questions about fasting.

5. ACTIVATE MORE ACTIVITY: Our bodies were not designed to sit for long periods of time. In 2006, Harvard Medical School put out the following statement: "Exercise helps prevent atherosclerosis." It also helps by "improving other

---

[17] For ebook readers, the link is here. For others, you can find it at my YouTube and Rumble channels. The title is *HUGE HEALTH RESET: The Benefits of Fasting | Idleman Unplugged.*

atherosclerotic risk factors, such as high blood pressure, diabetes, obesity, and stress."

Inactivity often leads to weight gain, and did you know that every pound of fat requires a few extra miles of blood vessels? That means more work for the body, especially the heart. *Lose the excess via activity and usher in better health.*

Ironically, the five points above are the best way to also ward off chronic stress, along with strengthening your walk with the Lord: "Casting all your care upon Him, for He cares for you" (1 Pet. 5:7).

Today's Choice, Tomorrow's Reward

There's been a video circulating on social media for the last few years asking, "What will the last 10 years of your life look like?" One side of the video shows an elderly man smiling and walking at a good pace, while the other side shows a man using a walker, obviously in distress. This is followed by another scene of an elderly man playing with his grandkids and lifting them up, compared to an elderly man being bedridden for the next 10 years. **It's vital that we choose the pain of discipline over the pain of regret.**

Don't focus on perfection; focus on direction. Begin by taking steps in the right direction, and when you fall, get back up and keep fighting. Health is a lifestyle, not a destination; it must be a priority.

Chapter Seven

I Almost Quit Too

Morgan Idleman: *Learning through the Landmines*

"The Pastor's Wife." It's how most people introduce us. Some have asked if that bothers me. I lean toward taking it as a compliment; how about you? Yes, we have our own identity. However, I learned long ago that my true identity is found in Christ, and Christ has called me to be a helpmate to this husband of mine, who just so happens to be a pastor. It is an honor to serve alongside him, and my privilege to be associated with him.

Fun fact: I didn't marry a pastor; I married a construction worker. It wasn't until eight years later that the Lord called us into full-time ministry, and we planted Westside Christian Fellowship in the Fall of 2010. I have often thought, "It's a good thing the Lord doesn't show us what's ahead." It turns out that a "lamp unto our feet and a light unto our path" truly is the best way (cf. Ps. 119:105).

I've only been at this for 15 years. While I certainly haven't mastered it, the Lord has definitely taught me a great deal along the way (usually by trial and error!), and I suspect He's taught you a thing or two as well.

In this chapter to wives, we'll look at some landmines that we face. The expectations. The loneliness. The criticism. The pastor's kids. The fishbowl. The list goes on and on. I knew nothing of this list until I stepped into these shoes, but I would soon find out what all of that meant and what came along with it. Truly, it seemed the Lord had the wrong girl if you asked me!

I didn't feel like your "typical" Pastor's Wife. I can't tell you how many times I've thought, "These poor people, they're stuck with me." I've got a past that would make anyone wonder why He chose me for this role. I can't cook. I can't sing. I don't play the piano, I don't have the gift of teaching, and I'm not a great hostess (I think number 1 has something to do with that.) Don't you need all, or at least one, for heaven's sake, of those qualities to take on this position? The funny thing is, First Timothy lists in great detail the qualifications for a pastor, but nowhere in Scripture is there an outline for a Pastor's Wife, other than what is outlined for *every* Christian woman. The Lord really had to do a deep work in me in those first few years and teach me about my identity being in Him and nothing else.

It's been such a journey. I can imagine you nodding your head in agreement. There has been heartache deeper than I could have ever imagined. And joy more abundant than I ever knew was possible. We have gone on adventures I'd previously only dreamt of and have had some of the most mundane of days in between. We have seen things I could have gone a lifetime without seeing, and we have seen things that we are forever grateful the Lord allowed us to have a front-row seat to.

We serve one of the most amazing groups of people you'll ever meet. It is truly an honor. And we have definitely made our fair share of mistakes. Anything good that has come from this ministry is by the pure grace of God. We owe it all to Him.

To be honest, I wasn't sure how to approach this chapter because I feel like I could write a whole book (Hmmm, maybe one day). But I need to keep it short and sweet. So, while I'd LOVE to gush about all the amazing aspects of ministry, because there truly are so many, I decided to just touch on what I've learned through a few of the landmines. I pray it will be an encouragement to you.

The Expectations

I can honestly say I've put more expectations on myself than I have ever felt from our congregation. It's been rare that I've heard hurtful words or seen hateful looks aimed at me. Sure, I've turned a corner or two and knew why "they" stopped talking. And from time to time, I've gotten the sense that someone was disappointed with me, that I let down their idea of what I "should be" or "should be doing," but overall, either people are *really* good at hiding their disappointment, or they truly accept me for who I am and what I am able to offer at this season in our ministry.

That said, it's still tough. I'd love to be all things to all people, but we know that's not practical for any of us. In the beginning, I wanted to be at every function, be able to meet with everyone who needed it, and attend everything I was invited to, etc. It took some time to learn that not only is it impossible, it would also be unhealthy. The ministry the Lord has called us to first is our husband and children. If you get one thing right, let it be this. **The alternative is ending up with a family who resents the church.**

Sometimes, we need to take a step back and take a look at what expectations we're putting on ourselves. Are they realistic? Are they from the Lord? Or are we holding ourselves to a standard no one is able to meet? Are they a distraction from the enemy to keep us defeated and deflated? I've been there. I still tell Shane about every six months that I'm not doing "this or that" right and how much farther along I should be by now. True, there is always room for growth, and it's my constant prayer that the Lord would show me how to be a better Pastor's Wife for the congregation He has entrusted to us. *But often, I beat myself up over things that man, or myself, have put on me.* If you get caught in that trap as well, take it to the Lord. Ask Him to shape you in this area and to show you what you're getting right (by His grace), what lies the enemy is feeding you, and any areas you can grow in. I've found He's faithful to answer those prayers.

Perhaps you are dealing with a member who is putting unrealistic expectations on you. In that case, you may need to gently remind them that you are only one person, and that your husband and children come first, that you really are doing your best, and that you'd be grateful if they would extend the same grace they would want you to extend if the roles were reversed. Those conversations are difficult, but what can be more difficult is not dealing with them, and it gets increasingly challenging the longer it lingers.

Switching gears: What happens when the expectations are reversed? Are there things you expect from your congregation that you need to let go of? I'll share about a time I had to do just that. I started to allow a root of bitterness to grow toward a few friends. Embarrassing, but true. I was so desperate for someone to come alongside our son during a difficult season. I reached out to different men (whom I know my son looks up to and that I trust), and asked them to pour into him, to mentor him. Nothing seemed to work out. My heart hurt. I held on to it, which was wrong.

Finally, I told Shane that I was struggling, and he reminded me, "It's not their responsibility, it's ours. People are busy, and they have their own lives." Which I know. But I also know the value in an older man coming along and discipling a younger man. And so, I had to prayerfully lay my expectations aside … including my expectation I had toward my husband of being "on my side" and going to some of the guys and saying, "Hey, can you help us bear some of this weight?" I had to repent, to lay it at the altar and say, "Lord, You know. You know what he needs. I trust You with him. It's not my job to try to force things or to have unrealistic expectations of people. Bring someone in Your time." Letting go of that expectation truly was freeing. Especially in light of realizing I can't be all things to all people, and neither can they.

That's just one example. I suspect you have similar things you could share. But listen, just as we wouldn't want people to expect things of us that we are unable to give, we also cannot expect it of them. My husband put it this way once, and it has stuck with me since that day: "This church is our life, it's who we are — it's ingrained into the very fabric of our being. It's like our 6th child, whereas the congregation is just coming to church when they can make it. Naturally, we will be the most invested, care the most, and want the best. The weight is on our shoulders."

How about your staff and volunteers? What expectations are you putting on them? Granted, some are good and healthy, and there needs to be a certain amount of valid expectations because you're leading the church, and we should strive to do all things with excellence. But you know what I mean. Are there any areas you need to take a look at? Back off from? Stop micromanaging? Is there anyone you need to apologize to? Do your staff and volunteers know how much you appreciate them? It might be time to encourage and thank them if it's been a while.

The Loneliness and Suffering Silently

Loneliness can be twofold. Some struggle with it because their husband has incorrectly prioritized his time. It can easily happen when they have so many demands. If you have expressed this to your husband and nothing has changed, may I suggest praying? I hear you saying, "Ok, Captain Obvious, is that all you've got?" But hear me out. What is *simple* is not always *easy*. Praying sounds like the simple answer, but it's not the easy one. It's not easy to practice the ministry of "zip your lip, stop nagging, and start praying" is it?

Stay with me here … we get to come before the God of the universe, the One who can hear and actually answer our cries for help. You can't convince me that if a Pastor's Wife, one who cares deeply about her marriage, her children, and her congregation, petitions the Lord (who cares even *more* about her marriage, her children, and her congregation) and asks Him to help her husband re-prioritize his time, that He won't hear that cry and answer that prayer. Sometimes, all it takes is us getting out of the way. **Sometimes we have to duck so the Holy Spirit can give our man a holy spanking.**

The other aspect of loneliness in ministry, and what I struggle with more so, is in the area of friendships. It's a lonely calling, amen? You want to have close friends within your congregation, but it's a weird dynamic. You can't open up with most because your husband is their pastor. At times, we suffer silently, don't we? And it's during these times that we learn Jesus truly is our best friend. The calling may feel lonely, but we're never alone.

Early on in our ministry journey, I remember an older woman telling me that I would be wise to find a friend outside of our church. While I didn't immediately understand why she would say that, I can now absolutely share the same advice with you, one hundred percent.

It can also get tricky when you've made friends with a staff member — lines get blurred. It's like being between a rock and a hard place when you have to take off the friend hat and address them from a leader's point of view. I've had to learn this balance time and time again. I'm telling you, there are parts of ministry I wish I could full-on run away from, and this is one of them.

Over the years, the temptation has been to not let anyone in. Honestly, I've given in to that temptation on a few occasions, especially after being hurt, but the Lord did not allow me to stay there for long. We aren't meant to build walls. Boundaries? Yes. Some guardrail for protection? Absolutely. But not full-on cinder block walls. *You know as well as I do that the walls we build to protect ourselves end up imprisoning us.* If you are struggling with this landmine, cry out to the Lord. Ask him to tenderize your heart toward people. Surrender past hurts. **Keep the boundaries, but let the walls down.** Pray for a sweet friendship or a mentor. He hears your prayer for community, and He will answer.

The Critical Hearts

It would seem weird for me to talk about being a Pastor's Wife without talking a little about the pastor I'm married to. At one of our 6 am worship services, I was singing and praying with my head down, but when I looked up, I saw Shane up front, both hands lifted high toward heaven. And as I scanned the room, I saw countless others doing the same. Or kneeling. Or sitting with heads in their hands, all drawing close to Jesus in their own way. My heart just about burst open at the seams!

Right then and there, I thought, "He has no idea what a good pastor he is." I know he always strives to do better, and he has not perfected it, but boy, I'll tell you, he will die trying. He is creating an atmosphere for us where we want more of Jesus. He is calling us to a deeper relationship with our Lord. He leads by example. Many see this on Sundays and Wednesdays, and during special services, but there are so many things behind the scenes that I'm privileged to witness.

I've seen the tears in his eyes for our congregation. I've seen him go help someone at the drop of a hat. I've seen him laugh with them, cry with them, pray with them, and contend for them. I've watched him challenge them, fast for them, fight for them, plead for them. I've seen him up at 3 a.m. praying, travailing, and crying out to Jesus for them. I've seen him mourn with them, rejoice with them, and comfort them. I've watched him work tirelessly for them, believe the best in them, confront them when needed, and stand by them. The love and compassion he has for our congregation are beyond words, and only the Lord could have given it to him. It is a true joy to watch, and it's a blessing to have a part in it with him. (I know, I'm biased. But I like to think that even if I weren't married to him, he would still be my favorite pastor.)

I have also seen the failures, the defeats, the hurts, and the disappointments. The faults, the blind spots, and the deficiencies. Like the rest of us, he is a work in progress. But Shane will go to his grave aiming to love Jesus more and more, and to point people to do the same. Like everything he's written about in this book, the enemy is always on the prowl, looking to take our husbands out … to steal their joy and destroy the ministry.

Despite all I just shared, the criticism still comes. And when it does, it hurts. It hurts me more so than it does him. He has much thicker skin than I do. I think it's so tough for me because I see him pour his heart out for people, pour his life out for people, and at times, miss family gatherings for people. So, when people criticize him, it's like a blow to my heart. I'd rather someone criticize me (which also happens). Now and then, I find myself wanting to say, "I give you access to my husband all day, all week, all month, for years, and we get criticism in return?" (Yes, that's totally my flesh coming out. It's wrong. I repent and move forward. But I thought you may as well know I deal with the struggles of the flesh just like you do.)

Please don't misunderstand: I'm not saying he has no room for growth. In fact, we both WELCOME constructive criticism from those whose hearts are pure and who are truly seeking to help. Thank God for that. It's how we all learn and grow. It's needed and necessary. What I'm talking about is the person who thinks they have the "gift of criticism" (good catch, you're right, there's no such gift!).

Have you been on the receiving end of critical hearts? The one who looks for every little thing they can find. The one whose intentions aren't pure, and whose motives are not of the Lord. It truly does make the encouragement that much sweeter, and thankfully, we get ten times more of that. But I've learned to be thankful for the criticism, even the downright rude things people say, because we all need to stay humble. It's good that we don't only hear praises. I didn't say it's easy, but I recognize that it helps keep me close to Christ! So, shout out to our haters … Thank you!

If you also trip over this landmine of having a critical heart, my encouragement is to let it go. I've walked in those shoes, and it's not a fun place to be. A critical, bitter Pastor's Wife is an oxymoron. If you feel that creeping in, petition the Lord to clear it out of your heart. Repent if necessary and begin to focus on the things you are thankful for. **A thankful heart has little room for a critical one.**

Deal with Offense Quickly

I'll never forget a conversation I had with my mother-in-law early on in ministry. I was asking her about this topic of offense, and she said, "Eventually you get to a point where you look over your shoulder (as if something flew right by you) and say, 'Was I just offended'?" It has been my prayer since that day that the Lord would bring me closer to that place, to let things roll off as quickly as they come, and not to allow the enemy a foothold in this area.

I mean, the enemy is just ruthless. Between *us* being offended and the congregation being offended *by us*, if we're not careful, this can quickly go from bad to worse. Whether it's something that was said, something that was done or wasn't done, maybe an invitation that wasn't extended, or a look seemingly given intentionally — there is always something, am I right? I've had to grow a backbone over the years, and the Lord has taught me HOW important it is to fight for unity. It will not come naturally, but it is so worth the effort to maintain it as best we can.

Of course, we can't go to everyone about every little thing or we'd be having meetings every week! We need discernment. I usually say if you truly can move on, do so. But if you just can't shake it and it's starting to grow a root of bitterness, then that offense needs to be addressed. I'm convinced that 9 times out of 10, people don't even realize they are offending you, and when you bring it to their attention, it affords them the opportunity to make it right.

I highly recommend the book, *The Bait of Satan,* by John Bevere. It should be required reading for anyone in ministry, truly a valuable resource. It teaches us how to biblically respond to offenses without letting them poison our hearts.

It seems the church has a revolving door; have you noticed? People come and people go. Sometimes the Lord moves them on, sometimes they move themselves on, and sometimes the enemy stirs up an offense that prompts them to move on. Some you watch leave as your heart breaks, and you so wish you could plead with them to stay. Others, you can see that it's the Lord moving them into a new season, and you support them 100%. You learn to love people fiercely while they are in your flock, but to hold them loosely, never knowing when you have to say goodbye, or if you'll even get the chance. **While they are with you, fight for unity.**

Swimming in the Fish Bowl

Then there's the fish bowl. Oh, the fishbowl. I'm learning to embrace it and swim around confidently in it. But most days, I feel like a fish out of water. I remember the days I didn't have people watching so closely. I think as Christians, we ALL have people watching us to some extent. But living it all day, every day, can be exhausting.

What is she wearing? Why is she so dressed up? Why isn't she dressed up? Why isn't she doing more? She has her nails done … is that the best way for her to spend her money? Is she teaching a Bible study? Why didn't she say hi to me? How does she discipline her kids? How often is she on social media? (Insert never-ending list here.)

We once had a woman write a Google review on the church based on the fact that I was wearing a ballcap. Never mind that it was on a Wednesday night and I was serving in our youth group, where it was completely appropriate attire. I remember thinking, "If THAT'S all you got out of tonight's service, Lord help you." It's crazy to me how critical people can be. She missed a powerful move of God that night because she couldn't see past what I was wearing. I could understand if it were a modesty issue. That's understandable. But a ballcap?!

Now, I am NOT saying I think I'm the center of everyone's attention. I really hope that's not your takeaway from that little paragraph. But I'm saying people watch, and sometimes judge, and sometimes comment — mostly to others, which would be called gossip where I come from.

One thing I've had to work through over the years is that you want to be "real." Your congregation needs to know you, know you care, know you're just a person in the lifeboat like the rest of them. No one wants a fake Pastor's Wife. (Good thing, because I couldn't fake anything if I tried!) However, I've found that there's a twist: If you're "too real," they lose respect for you as their Pastor's Wife. They want to know you're relatable, as long as that doesn't mean you have too many flaws.

If you try to walk that line of wanting to impress and "appear" more holy than you are, 1) people will see right through it, and 2) you will end up falling off the tightrope. I encourage you to consider getting to the point where you can say to your sweet congregation, "You got me, and I got you. Yes, I have flaws (quite a few!) Yes, you have flaws as well. Yes, we are all working out our salvation and being sanctified daily." Yes, there are women in our congregation who have been walking with the Lord much longer than I and have more wisdom than I do. While that used to intimidate me, I've since learned to embrace it. It's only pride that says, "I have it all figured out, I don't need counsel from anyone."

I'm so thankful for older women who have the wisdom to appreciate where the Lord has brought me, yet pray for me to go deeper. Yes, I am called to a high standard as a Pastor's Wife, but you are also called to that high standard as a

Christian. Let's encourage each other to grow in Christ and show grace when it's needed.

Married to the Pastor — Choose Your Hard

Real talk headed your way in 3, 2, 1 …

So, you're leading an amazing group of people who lean on you to help them with their marriages, families, and lives. Meanwhile, you are trying to foster a thriving marriage and raise kids who love Jesus through the ups and downs of life and ministry.

What about when *your* marriage is hanging on by a thread? What about when *you* don't like *your* husband? What then? What do you do when little foxes try to spoil the vine? I've got a good one for you: What about when you disagree with how your husband handles a church situation? (Don't leave me hanging; I know it happens to you, too.)

How do you lead women and help them thrive when you'd rather bury your head in the sand and quit? One simple mindset has helped me time and again: If we remind ourselves that we're not fighting against flesh and blood (although it may sometimes *feel* like it), we will realize that our husband is not the enemy. We have to put on the full armor of God and fight FOR marriage, rather than fighting IN it. **Your marriage IS your ministry.**

I praise God for the beautiful seasons, for the times Shane and I are in sync and on the same page. Marriage is such an amazing reflection of Christ and the church, and when it is functioning properly, with both people walking out their callings as husband and wife, submitted to Christ and to each other, there are few things more sweet than that.

But I also know firsthand how rough some seasons can be. We've had plenty in 23 years of marriage. Most recently, all in a period of 5 years, we went from a surprise pregnancy at ages 39 and 49, to me having postpartum depression, to Covid and the world going crazy, to our middle child having a serious injury, to Shane going through a dark season that he wrote about in this book, to me entering perimenopause. Any one of those things will test your marriage, not to mention them coming back-to-back. And I know some of you reading this have experienced much worse. Life can be so hard.

If there's one thing I've learned in 15 years of ministry, it's that the enemy is AFTER YOUR MARRIAGE. Letting down our guard in this area is not an option. But I haven't always lived that out. There have been times I allowed the enemy so much room in my marriage it's embarrassing. Unmet expectations, unsettled hurts, and unmatched bitterness took over, and I grew appallingly apathetic. It's amazing to me the depths the human mind can descend to when given the freedom. There have been times years ago (and we've shared this publicly, so don't worry, Shane isn't reading it here for the first time!) when someone would ask, "Where would you say your marriage is at on a scale of 1-10?" Shane would say an 8, and I would look at him in utter disbelief at how we could be living in the same marriage, as I would rate it a 3. Times when, *as a Pastor's Wife*, I would say, "Lord, I know there are no biblical grounds for divorce, so I am stuck here, but please, take one of us. I don't care if it's me or him, but one of us has got to go." Sounds horrible, I know, but it's where I was at, and it took a lot of time and prayer to get out of that pit.

Look, we can go to all the marriage conferences and do marriage counseling — those are good and God-given, but until we humble ourselves and fully surrender everything to Jesus, and allow Him to pick up the pieces, we are just grasping for the wind, and meanwhile digging a deeper hole.

Remember, we cannot force change in anyone else; we are not the Holy Spirit. What we *can* do is pray. We can own our part. Even if you're only 10% of the problem, own your 10%. We can control our responses. We can be sober-minded and self-controlled. We can let go of unrealistic expectations. We can ask the Lord to help us see our husband the way He sees him. We can allow him to lead (or encourage him to, depending on where your husband is at). We can spend time with our Savior, so we are ready for what the day may bring. We can kick the enemy out and get back to a thriving marriage. But it will take work, sacrifice, and compromise. Is that hard? Yes. But like Shane always says, so is living in an unhappy marriage, so choose your hard.

Five PK's — The Blessing and the Burden

The idea of my children being "pastor's kids" had always been a dreaded thought in the back of my mind. I've heard so many negative stories of PK's, most of them more like nightmares. It's not something any mother likes to think about: Her children rejecting the Lord and turning from the Faith. And it seems that PK's wander at an extremely high rate. What's a pastor and his wife to do? Hit their knees in prayer, that's what. It's our greatest defense and our only hope. We must also demonstrate love, grace, and forgiveness.

I'll never forget the time we visited a well-known church in Simi Valley, about 90 minutes south of our home, to meet with the pastor and get counsel before planting our church. As the service ended and we waited to be introduced, a couple of young kids in the seats ahead of us climbed up and started running across the chairs. Their dad grabbed one with one arm and the other with the other arm, looked around, and jokingly said, "Hey, whose kids are these, anyway?"

I'll give you one guess who their dad was … yes, the pastor of the church. At that moment, so many of my fears seemed to melt away. It was JUST what I needed to see and hear that day. It was such a glimpse of love, and joy, and grace in my mind. We've all seen kids run across the pews, and to know the PK's did it and were treated like all the other kids was a huge relief.

Again, (and I fear you'll think I'm exaggerating, or flat-out lying, or making up a group of people who don't really exist when I say this), our local congregation has been so supportive in this area. They truly love our kids and love on them week after week. It's been a rare occasion when I've felt someone putting pressure on our children because of who their parents are. You have no idea HOW grateful I am for that.

However, at times we have had to unapologetically remind people that our kids are just like the other kids in Children's Ministry in need of grace. Little humans trying to figure out their way through life just like the rest of us. Little souls who need Jesus just as much as anyone else. Just because the Lord called their dad to be a pastor doesn't mean they will be perfect. It can get confusing for them because the church is like their second home. They are comfortable there. And what does any kid do in a home they are comfortable in? They make themselves at home. So, they may find themselves doing things that other kids wouldn't do at church, or they may find themselves rebelling because of the pressure put on them.

They may not always be the best example among their peers. Do we aim for that? Absolutely! As all Christian parents should. But we are doing them a disservice if we put unrealistic expectations on them and make them feel they must "perform." No one should have to come to church wearing a mask, pretending to be someone or something they are not. We all have the freedom to come as we are. Our kids, your kids, we adults, we are all in this together. And when we are allowed to be real and authentic, that is how a true family is formed and how true change takes place.

Kids shouldn't run amok and get away with whatever their hearts desire, but church is also a training ground for them. Our ushers and teachers know they not only have our permission, but we also expect them to correct the kids, in love, if they're out of line. The kids know when someone cares. They see it in the eyes and hear it in the voice. It's rarely *what* we say, but *how* we say it.

Maybe you haven't thought of it this way before, but ministry is a sacrifice for the pastor's kids as well. They may deal with other kids not wanting to be their friends because they are intimidated by who their parents are. "She's the pastor's daughter; she's not allowed to do this or that." Or, "Oh, his dad is the pastor; I'll have to be perfect if I hang out with him."

As they get older, they may face things like intense peer pressure from those trying to get them to fall, just to get a good laugh out of it. "Ha-ha, I got the pastor's kid to _____ (you fill in the blank)." They also deal with the opposite — other kids *wanting* to be their friends *because* of who their parents are.

All that said, we teach our kids that it is a joy and honor to serve, and that the benefits far outweigh the sacrifices. Though there are some pitfalls, there are many, many blessings. They are privileged to see miracles happen before their very eyes. They get to take part in praying for the congregation and watch the Lord answer those prayers. They invest their little hearts into some of those prayer requests, and often, they even initiate the prayers. They get to tag along with Daddy to ministry events and watch him firsthand, ministering to and teaching people about Jesus.

It's a beautiful thing to stand next to my 20-year-old during worship and hear her singing loud and proud, pouring out her heart to the Lord. To hear our 18-year-old re-tell an account from the Bible. To listen to our 16-year-old quote the entire 23rd Psalm from heart. To see our 12-year-old helping a scared child in Children's Ministry. To watch our six-year-old make her way to the altar. There are some perks to being "dragged" to church all the time. They are learning and growing even if they don't realize it.

They are learning what it means to live a life sold out for our Savior, and we wouldn't want it any other way. Dying to self: It's the call for every believer, and the sooner they learn that, the better. So while the thought of raising PKs scares me at times, it also excites me, because I trust my Jesus with these babes. He WILL get all the glory due His name, and the enemy will not win.

It's possible that your congregation needs a gentle reminder, and it's okay to ask them to encourage your kids, love on them, invest in them, and pray with them. It is important to let them know they are not expected to be perfect and give them the freedom to fail, because they will fail regardless — they are human, and when they do, to lovingly help them back up and restore them in grace. To encourage their parents with words of kindness, point out the positives. And when an issue does arise that needs to be dealt with, remember how they want someone to come to them about their kids' faults or wrongdoings — all things done with love and grace.

Be Her — Seek Him

And then there are all the things that just fall under the category of "life." We have laundry to do, practices to attend, appointments, sickness, we go through childbirth (or infertility), we go through menopause, and we lose people we love. It's life. It's messy and hard and beautiful, and all the while, we are trying to navigate and lead a church and point people to Jesus.

About a year ago, I was reading in Proverbs, and I felt the Lord was saying, "Be her." Not as in trying to be someone I'm not, but be her … be that woman who is seeking hard after Jesus, who is in the Word, who is seeking His face. Be that woman who is applying scripture in her everyday life, who is a blessing to her husband, who is submitted to wherever the Lord leads. In a world that tells us to be all kinds of crazy things, just Be Her. Sit at the feet of Jesus. Stay close to His heart and His ways. It is then and only then that, when you feel like quitting, by His grace, you won't.

To Sum It Up — You Never Walk Alone

This is my theme song for Westside Christian Fellowship, for this ministry the Lord has entrusted us with, for all the years of His faithfulness. Every time I hear it, I either tear up or get a huge smile. It's Matt Redman's song, *Never Once*. Here are some of the lyrics, but I recommend listening to the whole thing:

> *"Standing on this mountaintop,*
> *Looking just how far we've come,*
> *Knowing that for every step,*
> *You were with us.*
> *Kneeling on this battle ground,*
> *Seeing just how much You've done,*
> *Knowing every victory*
> *Was Your power in us.*
> *Scars and struggles on the way,*
> *But with joy our hearts can say,*
> *Yes, our hearts can say,*
> *Never once did we ever walk alone,*
> *Never once did You leave us on our own,*

You are faithful, God, You are faithful."

Friends, He is faithful. We never walk alone. He's never once left us to do it on our own. He goes before us, He equips us, He holds us. May we never attempt to do this in our own strength!

If I can boil it down to one thing I've learned through the landmines, it's this: CLING. TO. JESUS. He has to be our everything. Does that make life perfect? No. But good luck trying to make it through any other way. He has to keep His reign as King of our heart and Lord of our life. Expectations, criticism, loneliness, fishbowl, marriage, kids, life … through it all, our eyes are on Him.

With all its ups and downs, the good, the bad, and the ugly, the blessings and the pain, there's nothing I'd rather be doing and no other cause I'd rather give my life to than to serve as a Pastor's Wife. **To see souls saved, chains broken, people set free, children having that "aha" moment, families restored, marriages back on track.** To watch people grow in Christ, going deeper in their walk, drawing nearer to Jesus. I'll take all of the difficulties if it means I can continue to have even a small part in all that. It's the biggest blessing and my joy to serve my husband and our congregation. I may have never seen myself in this role, but now I can't imagine myself doing anything else.

Well, there you have it … a small glimpse into my journey from sitting in the pew with my husband, to sitting in the pew alone, with my husband in the pulpit.

P.S. If you need a safe place to connect, I'd love to chat with you on my Instagram page at @idleman_theotherhalf.

Conclusion

The Conclusion of the Whole Matter

"Let us hear the conclusion of the whole matter: Fear God and keep His commandments, for this is man's all" (Ecclesiastes 12:13)

When pastors first begin their ministry, it's a time of excitement and enthusiasm. We are full of hope and optimism, but as time goes by, things can happen that dampen our passion, and doubt and despair can set in. Things such as missed opportunities, division in the church, and personal attacks result in bitterness and depression, as well as poor health. This can quench the fire that set us on this very special path.

When dreams die, we must remember that no matter what happens, we must keep moving forward. Why? Because God has called us, and God will sustain us. *We aren't here to simply wait for heaven; we are here to serve Him and to reflect His character.*

Rest in These Words: "He Has Called You"

I was at a point in my ministry when I had lost my passion. I went through the motions, but inside I knew something was off. I began to wonder if I had lost my way to the altar. My pursuit of God had become routine, rather than stimulating and exciting. To make things worse, I wasn't getting any younger, and my health was declining. I was struggling in every sense: physically, emotionally, and spiritually. Ignoring all the good that had resulted from my ministry, I was exhausted by all the negatives. I was ready to change course.

I used the idea of "landmines" to describe the major obstacles pastors face because they are hidden from sight but capable of utter devastation. We must remember that our enemy, Satan, sees the destruction of our ministry as one of his primary objectives. You have a calling from God and your ministry is precious in His sight. Your job is to persevere in your pursuit of Him.

Many years ago, a very old man who experienced a revival when he was younger, was asked why the revival ended. His eyes were filled with holy fire when he cried, **"When you lay hold of God, never, never, never, never let go!"** Let this be a warning to us as well, as a reminder to never let go.

Two Major Landmine Reminders

Two of the major landmines that can derail your ministry are pride and pain. Pride comes in many forms within ministry, and ironically, it is often related to the good things that we've done. Our pride impacts every aspect of our ministry, including finances, reputation, and influence. But that's not all it impacts: All the other people involved with your ministry will suffer if pride goes unchecked. *The spiritual weapons that combat pride are humility and repentance.* We won't win against pride unless we spend extended time in prayer, confessing our sins to God, and seeking forgiveness and restoration. When we do this, God will pour out blessings on us and our ministry.

The other big landmine is pain. Of all the things I underestimated going into the ministry, it was the amount of pain it would produce. Whether it's relational pain, criticism, burnout, disappointment in ministry, health issues, or personal struggles, they all take their toll. At times, the pain can seem unbearable.

When left unchecked, pain turns into discouragement, and we can easily become bitter. We must remember that God can use our pain to make us stronger. God can restore, refresh, and rebuild. God uses pain to make us more humble and better able to minister to the "walking wounded" in our churches. When you are feeling broken and discouraged, remember to spend time in praise and worship. It will get your focus off yourself and replace anxiety with peace in your heart.

A Renewed Focus on Mental Health through Physical Health

In addition to taking good care of ourselves spiritually, we can't forget the physical aspects of ministry. Our body is the temple of the Holy Spirit. We can build it up or tear it down depending on what we put into it and how we treat it. There is a proven connection between physical health and mental health. As pastors with incredibly busy lives and overflowing calendars, we might often put physical health at the bottom of our daily priorities. But that is not wise. I have personally experienced the benefits of a healthy diet and exercise, and I want to strongly encourage you to pay attention to this vital aspect of your ministry.

A Timeless Truth

My hope for this book is that it will give you strength and hope. If you are a pastor who is discouraged and questioning if this is God's plan for your life, you are not alone. You are not the first to experience this. Many other men of God have gone through this, and they have left us words of wisdom and advice from which we can profit greatly. But the primary place we will find wisdom and strength to help us navigate the challenges of ministry is God's Word, which is our spiritual food — it's a timeless truth.

Pursue God through every means available. Seek Him through prayer and fasting, honor Him through praise and worship, and obey Him through humility and repentance. God has called you to your ministry, and He will enable you to accomplish His will for your life: "We are hard-pressed on every side, yet not crushed; we are perplexed, but not in despair" (2 Cor. 4:8). **He will never leave nor forsake you.**

"Let us hear the conclusion of the whole matter: Fear God and keep His commandments, for this is man's all" (Ecc. 12:13).

Recommended Reading

Preaching and Preachers by D. Martyn Lloyd-Jones

Lectures to My Students by Charles Spurgeon

Disciplines of a Godly Man by R. Kent Hughes

The Sacred Anointing — The Preaching of Dr. Martyn Lloyd-Jones by Tony Sargent

Called to Lead by John MacArthur

Surviving the Anointing by David Ravenhill

Man of God — His Calling and Godly Life by Albert N. Martin

The Pastor — His Call, Character, and Work by the faculty and friends of old Princeton

www.ingramcontent.com/pod-product-compliance
Lightning Source LLC
Chambersburg PA
CBHW031451070426
42452CB00038B/701